The Dash Diet Made Easy

The Ultimate Beginner's Cookbook for a Low-Sodium Lifestyle with Mouth-Watering Recipes to Help You Reduce Your Blood Pressure 30-Day Healthy Meal Plan Included

By

MATILDA GRIFFITH

Table of Contents

Hello Reader,

I am the author, and I would like to tell you that I wrote the book with the greatest care possible, formatted to give the best experience, but if you encounter any problems (for example, grammatical errors or some inaccuracies), please let me know in order to improve the text as much as possible, and I will send you a file containing the updated version of the book and a bonus to thank you for your kind action.

Contact form:

<u>Click here to report the issue.</u>

Thank you

Introduction

When it comes to dieting, sometimes the hardest part is actually making the change. However, with a new understanding of healthy eating and keeping tabs on your calories, you can finally shed those extra pounds and see some major progress in your overall health. Recently, there has been a rise in the number of people suffering from conditions including high blood pressure, excess body fat, heart disease, and other illnesses. This Dash Diet cookbook offer you the perfect way to solve this issue because it fills your plate with healthy fruits, vegetables, and lean meats.

The Dash Diet, also called Dietary Approaches to Stop Hypertension, is a low sodium eating plan rich in fruits and vegetables. It is one of the only diet plans that has been shown in studies to lower blood pressure. It is based on the fact that almost all disease-causing inflammation in the body starts with what we eat, because most diseases are associated with chronic inflammation. This diet focus on Anti-inflammatory lifestyle and the idea is to have healthy eating habits, which will ultimately result in a healthy living.

The DASH diet is an essential way to lower blood pressure, reduce weight to lower risk of heart disease and other illnesses: cancer, diabetes, even dementia. They are not only tasty but also abundant in nutrients including vitamins and minerals that are beneficial for a healthy body.
Unlike other diets that focus on food restriction, this diet focuses on an eating pattern that promotes healthy living. This means that you eat a lot of fruits and veggies which help limit your intake of unhealthy that causes inflammation. The reason the Diet is used as a lifestyle is to replace all processed foods in your diet with more fiber-rich foods, like fruits and vegetables.

Several studies have demonstrated that the Dash Diet effectively improves blood circulation, as well as reduce weight and LDL ("bad") cholesterol. That is why it is recommended by the American Heart Association.
Eating a healthy and balanced diet is not an easy thing to do. But the Dash Diet can help you achieve your health goals and its recipes are easy to make as well. Without spending a lot of time in the kitchen, you may make tasty meals for the entire family.

Adopting a healthy eating pattern is essential to get rid of excess weight, lower blood pressure and other health problems that are associated with unhealthy foods. The Dash Diet is an essential way to kick start your new healthy lifestyle. It will help users get rid of the active inflammation and prevent further diseases. You will have more energy and feel better while your body is getting healthier every day.

What is Dash Diet?

The Dash diet is an eating regimen which has been scientifically proven to be more than twice as effective at reducing blood pressure levels when compared to a diet low in total fat. It utilizes the scientific principal of Load and Offset, which means that you will load your plate with whole grains, vegetables, and healthy proteins for six days out of a week and then fast for one day. This will help you maintain a healthy metabolic rate while also keeping your blood pressure under control. The Dietary Approaches to Stop Hypertension (DASH) study, a lengthy research project, served as the basis for the diet's main principles.

The National Heart, Lung, and Blood Institute created the Dash diet to combat high blood pressure and heart disease. 90% of Americans, according to the American Heart Association, are hypertensive without knowing it. High blood pressure is referred as "the silent killer" because it frequently stays untreated until your cardiovascular system has been harmed and typically has no noticeable symptoms.

The Dash diet's goal is to cut back on salt consumption. Also, it advises consuming meals high in magnesium, potassium, calcium and certain vitamins, like A, C and E. Researchers believe that the sodium in our diets causes hypertension by raising the blood pressure. The more salt in our diet, the higher our blood pressure rises. And this may result into a variety of health issues over time, including heart disease and stroke.

The two guiding concepts of the Dash diet are: 1) A low-sodium (or "balanced") diet high in fruits and vegetables, with a portion of lean protein sources (such as meat, poultry, fish, and eggs), but with over than 30% of the daily calorie intake coming from trans-fat; and 2) exercising to support cardiovascular health.

A healthy diet must contain less than 2,300 mg of sodium each day for good health. It is meant to be a low-sodium diet that provides more than the minimum recommended amount of potassium, calcium and magnesium. By reducing sodium in the diet and increasing potassium, phosphorus and magnesium intake, the Dash diet can help lower blood pressure. People's blood pressure can be lowered by an average of 5 mm Hg systolic and 2 mm Hg diastolic if they commit to this diet for two or more years. Also, a recent study discovered that reducing salt consumption is more closely linked to a decrease in systolic blood pressure than reducing saturated fat or total fat. Besides lowering blood pressure, the Dash diet may also help improve sleep and mental health. A review of clinical trials published in 2012 suggests that the Dash diet improves delta sleep scores and quality of life in people with hypertension compared to a diet that is lower in potassium and phosphorus.

The Dash diet was originally recommended for patients who were already on medications for high blood pressure, but it can be prescribed to healthy individuals as well. For lowering high blood pressure, it has grown to be one of the most well-liked regimens available.

There are several ways to administer the diet. Very frequently, it is administered as part of a weight loss plan as the Dash diet is often associated with low-calorie diets. In addition, some people follow the Dash diet to lower their blood pressure (alone), and still others use it to lose weight, improve mental health and sleep quality (a combination of the above).

Benefits of Dash Diet

The Dash Diet is one of the simplest methods to improve overall health and lose weight. Fresh fruits and vegetables, healthy grains, lean protein, and low-fat milk products are all abundant in this diet. The diet has been proven to influence the body in numerous ways such as:

a) **Healthy Weight Loss:** Studies show that eating healthy is the key to weight loss. There is evidence that the Dash Diet lowers blood pressure in obese people but also to improve their cholesterol levels and help them slim down. The Dash Diet will help you to lose weight more quickly than other diets because it has fewer calories but still contains all the nutrients your body needs to stay healthy.

b) **Improved Cholesterol Levels:** The Dash Diet works to lower your total blood cholesterol level by 1%. Also, it has been proven that the more closely you follow this diet, the more effective it is. So, by following this diet plan, you can reduce LDL and raise HDL numbers to a greater effect than eating a typical American diet. By lowering high blood pressure and cholesterol, you'll prevent heart disease from starting or worsening.

c) **Weight Loss:** The Dash Diet has been proven to help you lose weight. One study showed that when participants started eating healthy and exercised regularly, they lost weight and lowered their risk for heart disease. To some extent, eating healthy is key to weight loss. Such as reducing caloric intake and increasing physical activity.

d) **Improved Blood Pressure:** It has been demonstrated that the Dash Diet lowers blood pressure for people who have hypertension but also those with pre-hypertension. Eating healthy works to reduce your blood pressure; it also prevents heart disease and stroke. High blood pressure sufferers, pregnant women, diabetics, and those who are at risk of developing high blood pressure are all advised to follow the diet.

e) **Improved Blood Sugar Levels:** The Dash Diet will also help improve your blood sugar levels by eating foods that are low in carbohydrates (the key nutrients for maintaining normal blood sugar). It has been demonstrated to aid in weight loss, blood pressure reduction, and the prevention of heart disease and other chronic illnesses. By decreasing AGE levels, which are linked to a number of chronic illnesses, the diet has also been shown to help lessen the risk of developing diabetes.

f) **Better Cholesterol Levels:** With the Dash Diet, you'll enjoy higher HDL levels than those who follow a normal diet. It has also been shown to lower LDL cholesterol and triglycerides. It also helps raise HDL levels. Triglycerides can cause inflammation and plaque formation in arteries, which increases your risk for heart disease and stroke.

g) **Lower Risk of Chronic Diseases:** The DASH Diet is the greatest method to reduce your risk of developing chronic diseases. Your health will be improved in a variety of ways by eating nutritious meals. For healthy individuals, the Dash Diet has been shown to decrease blood pressure and cholesterol levels while warding off diabetes and heart disease. Also, this diet has been shown to enhance body composition, which lowers the chance of developing cancer and other chronic diseases.

h) **Improved Rest:** The Dash Diet improves sleep quality in a way that other diets fail to do. People who stick to the eating plan sleep better than those who don't, according to research. This may be because it improves mood and serotonin levels. The diet plan also helps reduce inflammation and oxidative stress, which can also cause trouble sleeping.

Dash Diet Food List with Low Sodium

1. **Vegetables:** you should aim for at least 45 percent of your meals to include a vegetable. such as: leafy greens, broccoli, kale or collard greens asparagus, celery and cucumbers, steamed spinach or green beans, Eggplant is also an excellent low-sodium option.
2. **Fruits:** apples, apricots, cherries, grapefruit, honeydew melon, oranges, tangerine, and Pineapple. Avocado is good because it is high in monounsaturated fat, protein and fiber. Bananas are also a good choice when eaten in moderation.
3. **Salad Greens:** romaine, iceberg, spinach, mixed greens, mix of greens such as romaine mix green with spinach. Kale mixed with spinach. Greek salad is an excellent choice. Grilled vegetables are another good choice such as broccoli, carrots and bell peppers. Due to their high potassium and fiber content and low calorie count, mushrooms are another excellent option.
4. **Soy/Pea Products:** tofu, edamame, tempeh, miso, shoyu (soy sauce), tempeh are high or good sources of protein.
5. **Legumes:** soybeans, lentils, beans include phosphorous and fiber. By interacting with cholesterol and increasing the level of HDL (good) HDL cholesterol, they aid in reducing the risk of type 2 diabetes. Grains are also good sources of protein and complex carbohydrates.
6. **Vegetable Broth**: is a good choice if it contains no added MSG especially those made from beans or vegetables should be consumed regularly.
7. **Nuts:** are also a good choice. Because they have little calories, monounsaturated fat, and protein, almonds are among the healthiest options. They include a lot of calories, monounsaturated fats, protein, and fiber.
8. **Whole Grain:** Quinoa is a good choice to include on the diet since it is high in fiber, calcium and iron. Brown rice, and buckwheat are excellent sources of complex carbohydrates. Oatmeal, and other wholegrain bread can be consumed daily.
9. **Drinks (water):** Hydration is key to staying healthy because it motivates people to eat more fruits and vegetables, which are the only healthy options people can consume when they are not eating a low-carb diet. Drinking water is important. You should take a lot of water when on a low-carb diet since it acts as a satiety aid, preventing you from overeating. Water is a weight-neutral fluid but it helps curb appetite and prevents overeating. Drinking water before meals helps people eat less.
10. **Meat:** should still be part of your diet on the Dash diet, but in moderate amounts per day. The amount of meat you can eat depends on your sex and age. For women, it is recommended that consumption be 1 to 1.5 ounces of lean muscle-meat per day while men should consume two to three ounces a day.
11. **Fish and Poultry:** You can eat fish and poultry, but in limited amounts. Fish portions range from 3 to 4 ounces, while chicken portions are about the size of a deck of cards. (about 4 ounces) or smaller than that. Studies have shown that consumption of seafood twice a week is beneficial for heart health, especially for younger women who are at risk for heart disease because they could probably develop high LDL cholesterol levels. By adding seafood and poultry to your diet, you can lower your saturated fat intake.
12. **Dairy:** The only dairy sources you are allowed to consume on the Dash diet are fat-free or 1% milk or yogurt, low-fat cheese, cottage cheese, part-skim mozzarella cheese or soy products. The best option is to consume fat-free or low-fat dairy products because they contain less saturated fat than full-fat dairy.

13. **Vegetable oil:** One serving of vegetable oil contains roughly 30 calories and 8 grams of total fat. It contains polyunsaturated fat, a healthy lipid that has been linked to a lower risk of heart disease. All best products include olive oil, canola oil, soybean oil and other types of cooking oils.

How To Get Started!

Eating healthy is hard. Finding the time and money for groceries can be difficult, and then there are all those recommended meals that are so expensive on a diet. But one of the simplest methods to eat healthier on a budget and lose weight is to follow the Dash diet.

The Dash diet is a great way to get started with healthy eating. It teaches the daily recommended amount of carbs, fats, proteins and even sodium that should be available in each meal. They are Dash also a great weight loss plan because it focuses on whole foods and low-glycaemic load foods. These are foods that digest slowly when they hit your bloodstream. This means the food will release its nutrients slowly, so your blood sugar and hunger won't spike.

The DASH diet's major objective is to wean people off of processed foods, sugar, carbohydrates, and salt since these substances can harm your health and cause issues including type 2 diabetes, cancer, and heart disease. The Dash diet also encourages eating healthy fats and not eating too many carbs – which are the two things our bodies burn the most related to energy.

The Dash diet is based on a vegan/vegetarian way of eating, but it doesn't actually require you to be vegetarian or vegan (which can be beneficial because it will cut down on processed foods and grains). You simply need to put yourself first and make sure you're getting plenty of healthy food. Though there are no specific timeframes or portion sizes – the main idea is that you're choosing lots of fruits and veggies, beans, nuts and whole grains. There should be a smaller amount of animal products and processed carbohydrates (like breads and pasta).

Now – let's talk about how to get started with this way of eating. The Dash diet won't be right for everyone, but if you've been looking for a healthier way to eat, this is a solid starting point. The Dash diet is also perfect for those who are looking for the whole foods approach to their diet so it's not too confusing. You can start by adding in Dash foods one at a time to your current diet – and see how it affects your weight and health when compared to not eating the Dash foods regularly.

Setting up your Dash diet is easy. You'll take a few min. to calculate your numbers. All you must do is find out your daily recommended number of calories for weight loss and maintenance. For women 2,000 and for men 2,500 should be the daily calorie intake for weight loss (and 1,800 and 2,200 should be the daily intake for maintenance). Then you select your food list and set your Dash diet meals up. Next, set up your individual meal plans based on your carbs, protein and fat intake for each meal.

Once you've set up your individual meal plans, select the right recipes to see how they come together. You'll see a description of what to add in and picture of the recipes itself. Choose your meals and set them up in recipe book, write down the ingredients you'll need to purchase and get cooking! By letting you choose your favourite foods the diet makes it easier for you to find foods that fit your numbers, bill and then pile on the nutrients. These are choices you'll typically find in supermarkets, health food stores and even regular grocery stores.

Now that you've picked out some new Dash foods to try –it's important to remember you don't have to eat every single meal all day. Here's how to go about incorporating them into your diet. You can try to eat a Dash meal twice a day – or you can just make sure you're eating them every day. The key is to incorporate them into your diet as much as possible.

In order to do this successfully, it's important not to get too strict with yourself. While the Dash diet does recommend staying away from processed foods and sugar, you don't necessarily have to give up all processed foods or sugar when you first start out. Because you're just starting out and have chosen to eat Dash diet foods – there's no reason to feel overwhelmed. You'll just be adding them into your diet – so stay calm and don't feel like you need to do too much at once.

To start eating the Dash foods consistently and keep track of your weight – you'll be amazed at how much healthier your body will become. Now that you know all of this, you're ready to start eating your new Dash diet foods. Here are some things you'll want to keep in mind when trying the Dash diet for the first time:

1. It's best to start out slowly. The Dash diet recommends starting out with one or two foods that you just try out here and there (you can start by eating them twice a week). If they make you feel great, go ahead and eat them every day.
2. The best time to start eating Dash diet foods is at breakfast and lunch. You can have a Dash meal for breakfast or lunch – and then for dinner you can eat what you'd like.
3. When you're first starting out on the Dash diet, just try to eat a few of the different types of foods. If any of them don't taste well to you, try not to be too hard on yourself. (remember – they were healthy even before they became popular). You can always experiment with other foods later.

Now that you have all of the information it's time to make the Dash diet part of your life, it's time to give this diet a try. At start, it's really important to stay accountable to yourself. When you make a commitment to eat healthy in a new way, it takes a lot of discipline – so if you're not used to this type of food, it may take some time. Just remember – you choose the Dash foods for a reason (since they are healthy for you) – if you don't like them, that's okay.

But what about if you do like the Dash foods? Great! Do not be distracted by what others are saying or doing. Do not allow people' opinions too much affect your decisions. (especially when it comes to trying out the new diet). It's up to you to know what you like, so stay strong in your beliefs and make smart choices.

In addition to making smart food choices – it's important to be patient with yourself (and not get discouraged). It isn't easy to change the way that you eat – but if you're determined, then you'll be fine. Always remember that it doesn't matter how other people are eating – the only thing that matters is how YOU are eating. If you're eating healthy, then you know all you need to know about how to eat.

Breakfast Recipes

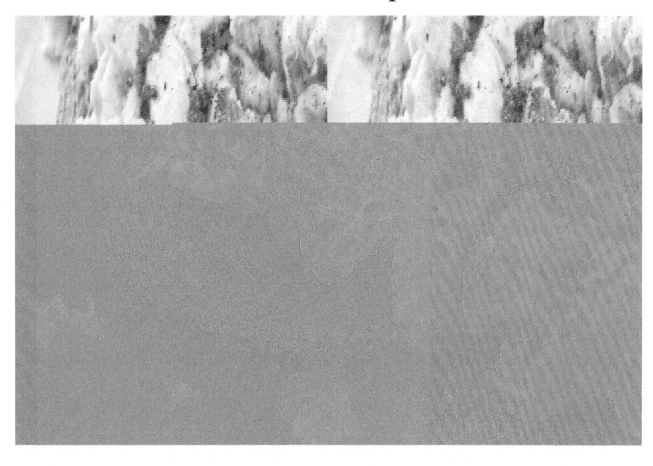

1.   Scrambled Egg on Whole Grain Toast

Preparation time: 5 minutes
Cooking time: 5 minutes
Servings: 1

Ingredients:
- Two big eggs
- Two tbsp low-fat milk
- One tbsp olive oil
- One-fourth tsp black pepper
- One slice whole grain toast
- Two tbsp chopped bell pepper (red, yellow, or green)
- One tbsp chopped green onions
- One-fourth cup baby spinach leaves

Directions:
1. Whisk eggs and milk in your container.
2. Warm up olive oil in your non-stick skillet on moderate temp. Add bell pepper plus green onions, then cook within one min till softened.
3. Pour egg mixture, then let it sit for a moment without stirring; then start gently moving the eggs around with a spatula.
4. When the eggs are almost fully cooked, add the spinach leaves and black pepper. Stir to combine until spinach is wilted and eggs are well-cooked.
5. Place your scrambled eggs on top of your whole grain toast. Serve.

Nutritional Values: Calories: 300; Carbs: 18g; Fat: 9g; Protein: 20g; Fiber: 3g; Sodium 280mg

2. Greek Yogurt Parfait with Honey and Nuts

Preparation time: 10 minutes
Cooking time: 0 minutes
Servings: 4

Ingredients:
- Two cups non-fat Greek yogurt
- One-fourth cup honey
- One cup mixed berries
- Half cup chopped nuts (such as walnuts, almonds, or pistachios)
- One-fourth cup chia seeds

Directions:
1. In four individual serving cups or glasses, layer the Greek yogurt, honey, mixed berries, and chopped nuts evenly.
2. Sprinkle chia seeds on top of each parfait. Serve.

Nutritional Values: Calories: 260; Carbs: 36g; Fat: 9g; Protein: 14g; Fiber: 6g; Sodium 50mg

3.   Overnight Chia Pudding with Fresh Berries

Preparation time: 10 minutes + chilling time
Cooking time: 0 minutes
Servings: 2

Ingredients:

- One-fourth cup chia seeds
- One cup almond milk, unsweetened
- Half cup Greek yogurt, low-fat
- One tbsp honey
- Half tsp vanilla extract
- One cup mixed fresh berries (raspberries, blueberries, strawberries)

Directions:

1. In your medium container, mix chia seeds, almond milk, Greek yogurt, honey, and vanilla extract. Stir well to combine. Divide it evenly between two jars.
2. Cover jars, then chill within 4 hours till chia seeds have absorbed the liquid and formed a pudding-like consistency.
3. When ready to serve, remove from the refrigerator and top each serving with a generous portion of mixed fresh berries.

Nutritional Values: Calories: 245; Carbs: 31g; Fat: 9g; Protein: 11g; Fiber: 12g; Sodium 103mg

4.   Mango, Kale & Greek Yogurt Smoothie Bowl

Preparation time: 10 minutes

Cooking time: 0 minutes

Servings: 2

Ingredients:

- One cup chopped kale, stems removed
- One big peeled & cubed mango
- One cup Greek yogurt, unsweetened
- Half cup almond milk, unsweetened
- One tbsp honey or to taste (optional)

Directions:

1. In your blender, combine kale, mango cubes, Greek yogurt, and almond milk. Blend until smooth and creamy.
2. Taste and add honey if desired for additional sweetness. Pour it into two bowls.
3. Decorate each bowl with your favorite toppings, such as chia seeds, nuts, sliced fruits, or granola. Serve.

Nutritional Values: Calories: 310; Carbs: 45g; Fat: 9g; Protein: 18g; Fiber: 9g; Sodium 95mg

5.   Whole Wheat Apple Cinnamon Pancakes

Preparation time: 15 minutes
Cooking time: 4 minutes
Servings: 4

Ingredients:
- Two cups flour, whole wheat
- One tbsp cinnamon, ground
- Two tsp baking powder
- One cup skim milk
- One big egg, lightly beaten
- Two tbsp unsweetened applesauce
- Two medium apples, peeled & grated
- Non-stick cooking spray
- Sugar-free maple syrup or light yogurt, for serving (optional)

Directions:
1. In your big container, whisk flour, cinnamon, plus baking powder.
2. In your separate container, combine skim milk, egg, plus applesauce. Mix it into dry mixture till smooth. Fold in grated apples.
3. Warm up your non-stick pan on moderate temp, then lightly coat using cooking spray.
4. Pour one-fourth cup batter, then cook within 2–3 mins till edges slightly set before flipping the pancake over. Cook within 2 mins till golden.
5. Repeat with rest of batter until all pancakes are cooked. Serve warm with sugar-free maple syrup or a dollop of light yogurt, if desired.

Nutritional Values: Calories: 275; Carbs: 52g; Fat: 3g; Protein: 11g; Fiber: 7g; Sodium 150mg

6.   Artichoke Egg Muffins

Preparation time: 15 minutes
Cooking time: 20 minutes
Servings: 6

Ingredients:
- Six big eggs
- One cup chopped artichoke hearts (canned and low-sodium, drained)
- Half cup red bell pepper, diced
- One-fourth diced cup onion
- Half cup shredded spinach
- One-fourth cup unsweetened almond milk
- One-fourth tsp garlic powder
- One-fourth tsp dried basil
- Black pepper, as required

Directions:
1. Warm up your oven to 350°F (180°C). Grease your non-stick muffin tin.
2. In your big container, whisk eggs, almond milk, garlic powder, basil, and black pepper. Add artichoke hearts, bell pepper, onion, and spinach. Stir until fully combined.
3. Pour it evenly into your muffin tin. Bake within 20 mins till egg muffins are set. Serve.

Nutritional Values: Calories: 110; Carbs: 4g; Fat: 7g; Protein: 10g; Fiber: 3g; Sodium 80mg

7.   Spinach Feta Cheese Frittata

Preparation time: 15 minutes
Cooking time: 27 minutes
Servings: 4

Ingredients:
- Eight big eggs
- Half cup unsweetened almond milk
- One tbsp olive oil
- One medium chopped onion
- Two garlic cloves
- Four cups baby spinach, washed & drained
- Two cup crumbled low-sodium feta cheese
- Half tsp black pepper

Directions:
1. Warm up your oven to 350°F (180°C).
2. In your big container, whisk eggs and almond milk until well combined.
3. Warm up oil in your big ovenproof skillet on moderate temp. Put onion plus garlic, then cook within 5 mins till softened.
4. Add spinach, then cook within 2-3 mins till wilted. Pour egg mixture, distributing evenly. Sprinkle crumbled feta cheese and black pepper on top.
5. Transfer skillet to your oven, then bake within 20-25 mins till frittata is firm. Cool it down, then serve.

Nutritional Values: Calories: 297; Carbs: 10g; Fat: 20g; Protein: 20g; Fiber: 2g; Sodium 560mg

8.   Banana Oatmeal with Flaxseed and Almonds

Preparation time: 5 minutes
Cooking time: 10 minutes
Servings: 2

Ingredients:
- One cup rolled oats
- Two cups water
- One-fourth tsp salt-free alternative (e.g., Mrs. Dash)
- One ripe banana, mashed
- Two tbsp ground flaxseed
- One-fourth cup unsalted almonds, chopped
- Half tsp cinnamon
- Optional toppings: fresh berries or sliced fruit

Directions:
1. In your medium saucepan, let the water boil.
2. Stir in rolled oats, salt-free alternative, and cinnamon. Adjust to low temp, then simmer within 5-8 mins till oatmeal is cooked through.
3. Remove from heat and mix in mashed banana. Gently fold in ground flaxseed and chopped almonds.
4. Divide the oatmeal into two servings and top each with optional fresh berries or sliced fruit. Serve.

Nutritional Values: Calories: 340; Carbs: 50g; Fat: 12g; Protein: 11g; Fiber: 9g; Sodium 15mg

9. Strawberry-Ginger Smoothie

Preparation time: 5 minutes
Cooking time: 0 minutes
Servings: 2

Ingredients:

- Two cups strawberries, hulled
- Half cup baby spinach, washed and drained
- One tbsp fresh ginger, grated
- Half medium banana, sliced
- Half cup unsweetened almond milk
- Half cup crushed ice

Directions:

1. In your blender, blend strawberries, baby spinach, grated ginger, sliced banana, unsweetened almond milk, and crushed ice till creamy. Serve.

Nutritional Values: Calories: 95; Carbs: 17g; Fat: 3g; Protein: 3g; Fiber: 4g; Sodium 90mg

10. Berry Quinoa Breakfast Bowl

Preparation time: 10 minutes
Cooking time: 20 minutes
Servings: 4

Ingredients:
- One cup uncooked quinoa, washed & strained
- Two cups water
- Half cup unsweetened almond milk
- One tbsp honey
- One tsp vanilla extract
- One cup fresh mixed berries (such as strawberries, blueberries, and raspberries)
- One-fourth cup nuts, chopped (such as almonds, walnuts, or pecans)
- One tbsp chia seeds

Directions:
2. In your medium saucepan, let water boil. Add quinoa, cover then adjust to low temp. Cook within 15 mins till tender. Remove, then let sit within 5 mins, then fluff with a fork.
3. In your small saucepan, warm up almond milk on low temp. Mix in honey plus vanilla extract.
4. Divide cooked quinoa among four bowls. Pour the warm almond milk mixture evenly over the quinoa. Top each bowl with an equal amount of mixed berries, chopped nuts, and chia seeds.

Nutritional Values: Calories: 317; Carbs: 46g; Fat: 11g; Protein: 11g; Fiber: 7g; Sodium 75mg

Lunch Recipes

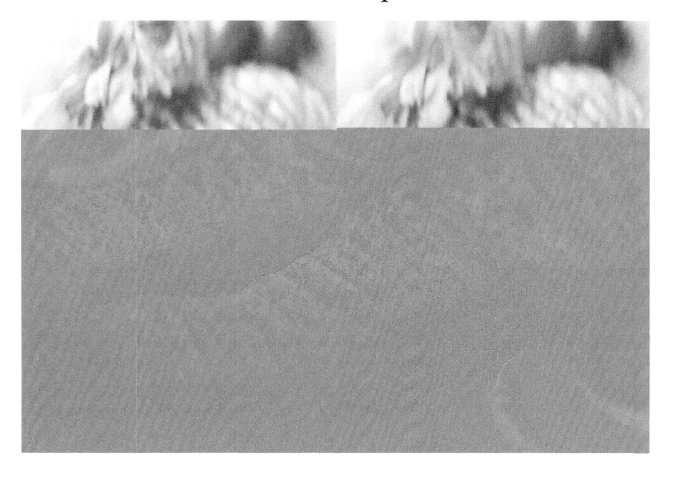

11. Roasted Salmon with Maple Glaze

Preparation time: 15 minutes
Cooking time: 20 minutes
Servings: 4
Ingredients:

- Four (six oz) salmon fillets
- One-fourth cup maple syrup, pure
- Two tbsp soy sauce, low-sodium
- One tbsp fresh lemon juice
- One garlic clove, minced
- One-fourth tsp ground black pepper
- One tbsp olive oil
- Two cups mixed greens (optional for serving)

Directions:

1. Warm up your oven to 400°F (200°C).
2. In your small container, whisk maple syrup, soy sauce, lemon juice, minced garlic, plus black pepper.
3. Put salmon fillets in your baking dish, then brush each fillet using olive oil. Pour maple glaze over each fillet, ensuring that they are coated.
4. Bake within 15 to 20 mins, basting the fillets halfway through with the remaining glaze from the bottom of the dish until the salmon is cooked through yet still moist and slightly pink in the center. Serve on a bed of mixed greens if desired.

Nutritional Values: Calories: 485; Carbs: 14g; Fat: 22g; Protein: 45g; Fiber: 0g; Sodium 320mg

12.   Pasta with Pistachio Mint Pesto

Preparation time: 15 minutes
Cooking time: 10 minutes
Servings: 4

Ingredients:
- Eight oz pasta, whole wheat
- One & half cups mint leaves, packed
- One-third cup pistachios, unsalted & shelled
- One-fourth cup parmesan cheese, grated
- Two garlic cloves, minced
- Zest & juice of one lemon
- One-fourth tsp black pepper
- One-third cup olive oil, extra-virgin

Directions:
1. Cook pasta as stated to package directions. Strain, then keep warm.
2. In a food processor, pulse mint leaves, pistachios, parmesan, garlic, lemon zest and juice, and black pepper until a paste-like consistency is achieved.
3. Slowly drizzle olive oil while your processor is running. Continue blending until the pesto becomes smooth and creamy.
4. Toss cooked pasta with the pistachio mint pesto until well coated. Serve.

Nutritional Values: Calories: 448; Carbs: 44g; Fat: 23g; Protein: 14g; Fiber: 6g; Sodium 47mg

13.   Spicy Shrimp and Avocado Salad

Preparation time: 15 minutes
Cooking time: 4 minutes
Servings: 4

Ingredients:
- One-pound big shrimp, peeled & deveined
- One tbsp olive oil
- Half tbsp low-sodium Cajun seasoning
- Two avocados, cubed
- Half small red onion, thinly sliced
- One-fourth cup chopped cilantro
- Juice of one lime
- One-fourth tsp black pepper

Directions:
1. In your medium container, mix shrimp, oil plus Cajun seasoning.
2. Warm up your grill on moderate-high temp. Cook shrimp within 2 mins per side till cooked through.
3. In your big container, mix onion, avocados, cilantro, plus lime juice. Add cooked shrimp, then toss again. Flavor it with black pepper. Serve.

Nutritional Values: Calories: 340; Carbs: 14g; Fat: 22g; Protein: 24g; Fiber: 7g; Sodium 190mg

14.   Turkey Swiss Lettuce Wraps

Preparation time: 10 minutes
Cooking time: 10 minutes
Servings: 4

Ingredients:

- One-pound low-sodium, lean ground turkey
- One tbsp olive oil
- One-fourth each of cup diced onion, red bell pepper & mushrooms
- Four slices low-sodium Swiss cheese, halved
- Eight large lettuce leaves, washed and dried (preferably iceberg, romaine or butter lettuce)
- One small avocado, sliced thinly

Directions:

1. Warm up your olive oil in your skillet on moderate temp. Put onions, bell pepper, plus mushrooms, then sauté within 3 mins till soften.
2. Add ground turkey and break it up with a spatula. Cook within 7 mins till fully cooked.
3. Lay out the lettuce leaves on a clean surface or plate. Place about two tablespoons of the cooked turkey mixture on each leaf.
4. Top each wrap using half of Swiss cheese slice plus a few slices of avocado. Add optional toppings if desired, such as cherry tomatoes or black olives.
5. Carefully fold the lettuce leaves over the filling, tucking in the edges to form a wrap. Serve.

Nutritional Values: Calories: 342; Carbs: 10g; Fat: 23g; Protein: 26g; Fiber: 5g; Sodium 300mg

15.　Citrus Quinoa Stuffed Peppers

Preparation time: 15 minutes
Cooking time: 30 minutes
Servings: 4

Ingredients:
- Four bell peppers, assorted colors, remove tops & seeded
- One cup cooked quinoa
- Half cup chopped cucumber
- Half cup halved cherry tomatoes
- One-fourth cup diced red onion
- One-fourth cup chopped fresh cilantro
- One-fourth cup fresh orange juice
- One tbsp lemon juice, fresh
- Two tbsp olive oil
- salt & pepper, as required

Directions:
1. Warm up your oven to 350°F (180°C).
2. In your big container, mix quinoa, chopped cucumber, cherry tomatoes, red onion, plus cilantro.
3. In your small container, whisk orange juice, lemon juice, oil, salt, plus pepper. Pour it over quinoa mixture, then toss it well.
4. Divide citrus quinoa mixture evenly among the four cleaned and cored bell peppers.
5. Put stuffed bell peppers in your baking dish, then cover with aluminum foil to keep them upright while cooking. Bake for 30 mins till peppers are tender. Serve.

Nutritional Values: Calories: 240; Carbs: 36g; Fat: 9g; Protein: 7g; Fiber: 6g; Sodium 50mg

16. Veggie Hummus Pita Sandwich

Preparation time: 10 minutes
Cooking time: 0 minutes
Servings: 2

Ingredients:
- Two pita breads, whole wheat
- Half cup hummus, low-sodium
- One cup shredded lettuce
- One small thinly sliced cucumber
- One small thinly sliced red bell pepper
- Half cup grated carrots
- One-fourth cup sliced red onion

Directions:
1. Cut each pita bread in half to create 4 pockets. Carefully open each pita pocket and spread the inside with a generous layer of low-sodium hummus.
2. In each pita, layer lettuce, cucumber slices, red bell pepper slices, grated carrots, and sliced red onion. Serve.

Nutritional Values: Calories: 325; Carbs: 50g; Fat: 9g; Protein: 13g; Fiber: 9g; Sodium 280mg

17.   Brown Rice Vegetable Stir-Fry Bowl

Preparation time: 15 minutes
Cooking time: 7 minutes
Servings: 4

Ingredients:

- Two cups cooked brown rice
- One cup broccoli floret
- One cup bell pepper, thinly sliced (assorted colors)
- One cup carrot, julienned
- One cup trimmed sugar snap pea
- One cup sliced mushroom
- Three garlic cloves, minced
- One-fourth cup soy sauce, low-sodium
- Two tbsp each of sesame oil & rice vinegar
- ground black pepper, as required

Directions:
In your big skillet, warm up sesame oil on moderate-high temp. Put garlic, then cook within one min till fragrant.

1. Put broccoli, bell peppers, carrots, sugar snap peas, and mushrooms. Stir-fry within 5 mins till vegetables are tender.
2. Combine low-sodium soy sauce plus rice vinegar in your small container. Pour over vegetables, then continue to cook for another minute or two. Flavor it with black pepper. Serve warm with cooked brown rice.

Nutritional Values: Calories: 340; Carbs: 55g; Fat: 9g; Protein: 9g; Fiber: 6g; Sodium 300mg

18.   Lemon Herb Salmon with Asparagus

Preparation time: 15 minutes
Cooking time: 15 minutes
Servings: 4

Ingredients:

- Four (six oz) salmon fillets
- One pound asparagus, trimmed
- Two tbsp olive oil
- Two tbsp fresh lemon juice
- Zest of one lemon
- Two minced garlic cloves
- One tbsp chopped dill, fresh
- One tbsp chopped parsley, fresh
- Ground black pepper, as required

Directions:

1. Warm up your oven to 400°F (200°C).
2. In your small container, whisk olive oil, lemon zest, juice, garlic, dill, parsley, and black pepper.
3. Put salmon fillets on your parchment-lined baking sheet. Arrange asparagus around the salmon fillets. Drizzle the lemon herb mixture evenly.
4. Bake within 12-15 mins till salmon flakes easily. Plate the salmon and asparagus, spooning any remaining pan juices over top before serving.

Nutritional Values: Calories: 379; Carbs: 5g; Fat: 23g; Protein: 37g; Fiber: 2g; Sodium 102mg

19. Grilled Veggie Skewers with Pesto

Preparation time: 20 minutes
Cooking time: 10 minutes
Servings: 4

Ingredients:
- Two cups basil leaves, fresh
- Two garlic cloves, minced
- One-fourth cup Parmesan cheese, grated
- Three tbsp walnuts, unsalted
- One-fourth cup olive oil, extra-virgin
- One tbsp lemon juice, fresh
- Ground black pepper, as required
- Two bell peppers (red, yellow or green), sliced into one" pieces
- One big zucchini, sliced into one" rounds
- Twelve cherry tomatoes
- One small red onion, sliced

Directions:
1. In your food processor, blend basil leaves, garlic, Parmesan, walnuts, olive oil, plus lemon juice till smooth. Flavor it using black pepper. Put aside.
2. Preheat grill to medium heat. Thread the bell peppers, zucchini, cherry tomatoes, plus red onion onto your skewers alternately.
3. Grill within 10 mins till vegetables are tender, flipping often. Remove, then place on your serving plate. Drizzle pesto sauce before serving.

Nutritional Values: Calories: 280; Carbs: 16g; Fat: 21g; Protein: 8g; Fiber: 4g; Sodium 92mg

20. Light Cauliflower-Mushroom Risotto

Preparation time: 15 minutes
Cooking time: 30 minutes
Servings: 4

Ingredients:

- Four cups cauliflower rice
- One tbsp olive oil
- One small diced yellow onion
- Two minced garlic cloves
- Eight oz mushrooms, sliced (white button or cremini)
- One cup arborio rice
- Four cups vegetable broth, low-sodium
- One-third cup Parmesan cheese, grated
- One-fourth cup chopped fresh parsley
- Salt & pepper, as required

Directions:

1. In your big skillet, warm up olive oil on moderate temp. Put onion, then sauté within 5 mins till softened.
2. Put garlic plus mushrooms, then cook within 5 to 7 mins till mushrooms are tender.
3. Stir in arborio rice, mixing well with the vegetables. Add one cup of low-sodium vegetable broth and cook until absorbed, stirring constantly.
4. Continue adding the vegetable broth in one-cup increments, allowing each addition to absorb till rice is tender but still has some bite (around 20 mins).
5. Mix in cauliflower rice, then cook within 5 to 7 mins till softened. Remove, then mix in grated Parmesan cheese plus fresh parsley. Flavor it using salt plus pepper. Serve.

Nutritional Values: Calories: 380; Carbs: 61g; Fat: 8g; Protein: 15g; Fiber: 6g; Sodium 220mg

Dinner Recipes

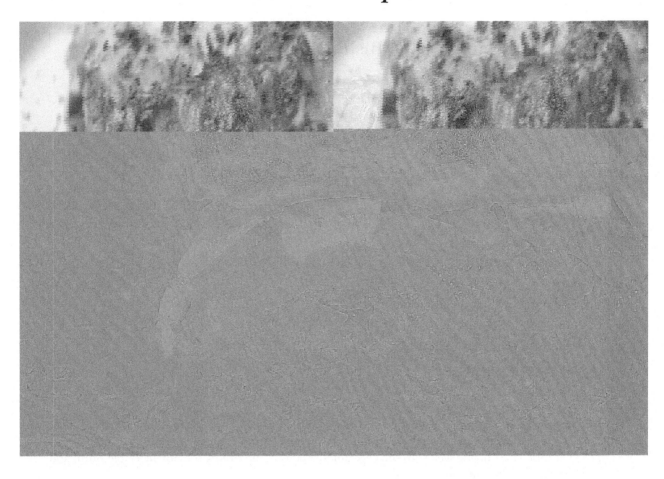

21. Vegetarian Lasagna

Preparation time: 30 minutes
Cooking time: 1 hour & 5 minutes
Servings: 8

Ingredients:
- Twelve low-sodium whole wheat lasagna noodles
- Two cups fresh spinach, chopped
- One cup broccoli, finely chopped
- One medium zucchini, sliced
- Two cups sliced mushrooms
- One big chopped onion
- Two minced garlic cloves
- Fifteen oz low-sodium ricotta cheese
- One-fourth cup Parmesan cheese, grated
- Two cups low-sodium mozzarella cheese, shredded
- Twenty-four oz low-sodium marinara sauce
- Olive oil, for sautéing

Directions:
1. Warm up your oven to 375°F (190°C). Cook lasagna noodles as stated to package instructions. Put aside.
2. In your big skillet, warm up a little olive oil on moderate temp. Put onion plus garlic, then sauté within 5 mins till softened.
3. Put spinach, broccoli, zucchini, plus mushrooms, then cook within 10 mins till vegetables are tender, stirring occasionally.
4. In your container, combine ricotta, Parmesan, plus half of mozzarella cheese.
5. To assemble lasagna, spread marinara sauce on your 13x9" baking dish. Layer with lasagna noodles, ricotta mixture, vegetables, and sauce. Repeat layers until all ingredients are used up.
6. Add remaining mozzarella cheese, then sprinkle Parmesan.
7. Cover using foil, bake within 30 mins, uncover, then bake again within 20 mins till golden. Cool it down, then serve.

Nutritional Values: Calories: 356; Carbs: 45g; Fat: 13g; Protein: 23g; Fiber: 7g; Sodium 330mg

22.   Baked Salmon with Quinoa and Vegetables

Preparation time: 15 minutes
Cooking time: 35 minutes
Servings: 4

Ingredients:
- Four (six oz each) salmon fillets, skinless
- One cup quinoa, washed & strained
- Two cups low-sodium vegetable broth
- Half tsp olive oil
- One tsp lemon zest
- Two tbsp lemon juice, freshly squeezed
- One-fourth tsp black pepper, freshly ground
- Two cups broccoli florets
- Two cups carrot sticks
- Two cups cherry tomatoes, halved

Directions:
1. Warm up your oven to 400°F (200°C).
2. Line your baking sheet using parchment paper, then put salmon fillets with some space between each fillet.
3. In your medium saucepan, boil quinoa plus broth to a boil on high temp. Adjust to low temp, cover, then simmer within 15 mins till quinoa is cooked.
4. Meanwhile, rub each salmon fillet with olive oil, zest, lemon juice, plus black pepper. Bake within 15 mins till salmon flakes easily.
5. For steamed vegetables, steam broccoli florets and carrot sticks within 5 mins till tender.
6. To assemble, divide quinoa among four plates; top each portion of quinoa with baked salmon fillet; serve steamed vegetables on the side alongside cherry tomatoes.

Nutritional Values: Calories: 569; Carbs: 45g; Fat: 23g; Protein: 50g; Fiber: 7g; Sodium 310mg

23.   Chili Lime Grilled Tofu with Avocado Salsa

Preparation time: 15 minutes
Cooking time: 20 minutes
Servings: 4

Ingredients:

- Fourteen oz firm tofu, pressed and cut into squares
- Two tbsp soy sauce, low-sodium
- One tbsp lime juice
- One tbsp olive oil
- One tbsp apple cider vinegar
- One garlic clove, minced
- One tsp low-sodium chili powder
- For the Avocado Salsa:
- Two ripe avocados, diced
- One cup halved cherry tomato
- Half cup chopped red onion
- One-fourth cup fresh chopped cilantro
- Juice of one lime
- Salt & pepper, as required

Directions:

1. In a shallow dish, whisk together soy sauce, lime juice, oil, apple cider, minced garlic, chili powder, and cayenne pepper.
2. Add pressed tofu squares to the marinade, then toss it well. Marinate within 15 mins.
3. Preheat a grill or grill pan. Once hot, cook tofu within 5 mins on each side till grill marks appear.
4. While the tofu is grilling, prepare the avocado salsa by combining diced avocados, cherry tomatoes, red onion, cilantro, and lime juice in your container. Gently mix and flavor it with salt plus pepper.
5. Once tofu is cooked, cool it slightly, then serve with avocado salsa on top or on the side.

Nutritional Values: Calories: 320; Carbs: 20g; Fat: 24g; Protein: 14g; Fiber: 8g; Sodium 250mg

24. Vegetable Pasta Primavera

Preparation time: 20 minutes
Cooking time: 25 minutes
Servings: 4

Ingredients:
- Eight oz spaghetti, whole-wheat
- One tbsp olive oil
- Two garlic cloves, minced
- One thinly sliced each of yellow squash, zucchini & red bell pepper
- One cup cherry tomatoes, halved
- One-fourth cup chopped fresh basil
- Juice of half a lemon
- Black pepper, as required

Directions:
1. Boil your big pot of water and cook spaghetti as stated to package instructions till tender. Strain, then put aside.
2. In your big skillet, warm up olive oil on moderate temp. Put garlic, then cook within 1 min till fragrant.
3. Add yellow squash, zucchini, plus bell pepper, then cook within 5 mins till vegetables are tender.
4. Add cherry tomatoes, then cook within 3 mins till tomatoes slightly soften.
5. Stir in cooked spaghetti, chopped basil, and lemon juice; toss gently to combine with vegetables. Season with black pepper. Serve.

Nutritional Values: Calories: 274; Carbs: 48g; Fat: 7g; Protein: 10g; Fiber: 8g; Sodium 17mg

25.   Shrimp Stir-Fry with Brown Rice

Preparation time: 15 minutes
Cooking time: 20 minutes
Servings: 4

Ingredients:

- One cup uncooked brown rice
- Two cups water
- One-pound raw shrimp, peeled and deveined
- Two cups mixed vegetables (such as bell peppers, carrots, snow peas, and broccoli)
- Three garlic cloves, minced
- One-fourth cup soy sauce, low-sodium
- Two tbsp oyster sauce
- One tbsp cornstarch mixed with 3 tablespoons cold water
- One tbsp olive oil
- ground black pepper, as required

Directions:

1. Cook brown rice according to package instructions using the 2 cups of water.
2. Meanwhile, warm up oil in your big skillet on moderate-high temp. Put garlic, then cook within 30 seconds till fragrant.
3. Put mixed vegetables, then cook within 5 mins till tender. Put shrimp, then cook within 3-5 mins till shrimp is pink and cooked through.
4. In your small container, mix low-sodium soy & oyster sauce, plus cornstarch mixture together. Pour it in your skillet. Stir everything together, then cook within one min till sauce thickens.
5. Serve shrimp stir-fry over cooked brown rice, seasoned with freshly ground black pepper.

Nutritional Values: Calories: 390; Carbs: 49g; Fat: 7g; Protein: 33g; Fiber: 6g; Sodium 390mg

26.   Turkey and Vegetable Skillet with Quinoa

Preparation time: 15 minutes
Cooking time: 33 minutes
Servings: 4

Ingredients:

- One cup uncooked quinoa, washed & strained
- Two cups low-sodium chicken broth
- One tbsp olive oil
- One-pound lean ground turkey
- One small chopped onion
- Two minced garlic cloves
- One chopped zucchini
- One chopped yellow squash
- One chopped red bell pepper
- One cup cherry tomato, halved
- One tsp dried oregano

Directions:

1. In your medium saucepan, combine quinoa plus broth, then let it boil on high temp. Adjust to low temp, cover, then simmer within 15 mins till quinoa is cooked. Fluff with a fork.
2. Meanwhile, warm up olive oil in your big skillet on moderate temp. Add ground turkey, then cook within 5-6 mins till browned, crumbling it.
3. Add onion plus garlic, then cook within 3 mins till onion is tender.
4. Stir in zucchini, yellow squash, red bell pepper, cherry tomatoes, plus dried oregano. Cook within 10 mins till vegetables are tender.
5. Add cooked quinoa to the skillet with turkey and vegetables mixture; stir well so everything is evenly distributed.
6. Serve warm.

Nutritional Values: Calories: 424; Carbs: 44g; Fat: 14g; Protein: 32g; Fiber: 6g; Sodium 214mg

27.   White Bean and Kale Stew

Preparation time: 15 minutes
Cooking time: 30 minutes
Servings: 6

Ingredients:

- One tbsp olive oil
- One big onion, diced
- Two minced garlic cloves
- Four cups vegetable broth, low-sodium
- Two (fifteen oz each) cans low-sodium white beans, washed & strained
- One bunch kale, stems removed and leaves chopped
- Two tsp dried thyme
- Black pepper, as required

Directions:

1. Warm up olive oil in your pot on moderate temp. Put onion, then cook within 5 mins till softened.
2. Mix in garlic, then cook within one min.
3. Pour broth, add beans, then let it boil. Adjust to a simmer, cover, then cook within 20 mins.
4. Stir in chopped kale leaves plus dried thyme, then cook within 10 mins till kale is tender.
5. Flavor with black pepper. Serve.

Nutritional Values: Calories: 236; Carbs: 37g; Fat: 5g; Protein: 14g; Fiber: 8g; Sodium 263mg

28. Sesame Ginger Salmon with Bok Choy

Preparation time: 15 minutes
Cooking time: 25 minutes
Servings: 4

Ingredients:
- Four (six oz) salmon fillets
- One tbsp low-sodium soy sauce
- One tbsp sesame oil
- Three minced garlic cloves
- One tbsp grated ginger
- Two tbsp fresh lime juice
- One tsp honey
- One bunch bok choy, washed and separated into individual leaves
- Two finely chopped green onions
- One tbsp sesame seeds

Directions:
1. Warm your oven to 400°F (204°C).
2. In your small container, mix soy sauce, oil, garlic, grated ginger, lime juice, and honey. Put aside.
3. Put salmon fillets on your parchment-lined baking sheet.
4. Brush each salmon fillet using sesame ginger marinade, reserving some marinade for the bok choy.
5. Bake salmon within 20 mins till it flakes easily.
6. Meanwhile, steam bok choy in your steamer within 5 mins till tender.
7. Place steamed bok choy on your plate, then drizzle using rest of sesame ginger marinade. Remove salmon, then place it on bok choy. Garnish using green onions plus sesame seeds. Serve.

Nutritional Values: Calories: 350; Carbs: 7g; Fat: 19g; Protein: 37g; Fiber: 2g; Sodium 420mg

29. Penne Arrabiata with Turkey Meatballs

Preparation time: 20 minutes
Cooking time: 40 minutes
Servings: 4

Ingredients:
- Eight oz whole-wheat penne pasta
- One-pound lean ground turkey
- One-fourth cup fresh parsley, chopped
- One-fourth cup Parmesan cheese, grated
- One-fourth cup whole-wheat breadcrumbs
- One egg, lightly beaten
- Two tsp olive oil
- One small onion, diced
- Two minced garlic cloves
- One tsp dried red pepper flakes
- Twenty-eight oz no-salt-added crushed tomatoes
- One-fourth tsp black pepper

Directions:
Cook penne pasta as stated to package instructions in unsalted water till tender. Strain, then put aside.
1. In your container, combine ground turkey, parsley, Parmesan cheese, breadcrumbs, and beaten egg. Shape into small meatballs.
2. Warm up olive oil in your big skillet on moderate temp. Add meatballs, then cook within 12-15 mins till browned, mixing occasionally for even browning. Remove meatballs, then put aside.
3. In your same skillet, add onion, then cook within 5 mins till softened. Add minced garlic plus pepper flakes, then cook within one min.
4. Mix in no-salt-added crushed tomatoes, plus black pepper. Let it simmer, put cooked meatballs, then cook on low heat for an additional 15 mins. Serve the arrabiata sauce over cooked penne pasta.

Nutritional Values: Calories: 449; Carbs: 56g; Fat: 12g; Protein: 32g; Fiber: 11g; Sodium 225mg

30. Sweet Potato Cauliflower Curry

Preparation time: 15 minutes
Cooking time: 35 minutes
Servings: 4

Ingredients:
- One big head cauliflower, cut into florets
- Two medium sweet potatoes, peeled & cubed
- One medium chopped onion
- Two garlic cloves, minced
- One" grated fresh ginger
- One tbsp no-salt-added curry powder
- One tsp turmeric, ground
- Half tsp cumin, ground
- One-fourth tsp coriander, ground
- One-fourth tsp cinnamon, ground
- One cup unsweetened canned coconut milk
- Two cups vegetable broth, low-sodium
- Two tbsp olive oil

Directions:
1. In your big pot, warm up olive oil over on moderate temp. Put onion, then cook within 3 mins till softened.
2. Put minced garlic plus grated ginger, then stir for a minute more.
3. Mix in curry powder, turmeric, cumin, coriander, plus cinnamon. Cook within one min to allow the spices to become fragrant.
4. Mix in cauliflower florets and cubed sweet potatoes.
5. Pour the coconut milk and low-sodium vegetable broth into the pot. Let it boil on high temp.
6. Once boiling, adjust to low temp, then simmer covered within 25 mins till vegetables are tender. Serve.

Nutritional Values: Calories: 280; Carbs: 30g; Fat: 15g; Protein: 6g; Fiber: 7g; Sodium 150mg

Fish & Seafood Recipes

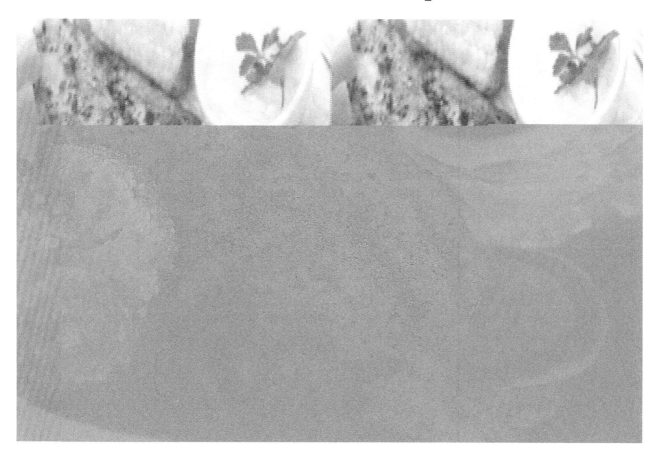

31.   Tilapia Broccoli Platter

Preparation time: 10 minutes
Cooking time: 20 minutes
Servings: 4

Ingredients:
- Four (about one pound) tilapia fillets
- One big head of broccoli, cut into florets
- Two tbsp olive oil
- One tbsp fresh lemon juice
- Half tsp each of garlic powder & onion powder
- One-fourth tsp each of black pepper & paprika

Directions:
1. Warm up your oven to 375°F (190°C).
2. Prepare your baking sheet using parchment paper, then add tilapia fillets plus broccoli
3. In your small container, mix oil, lemon juice, garlic & onion powder, black pepper, plus paprika.
4. Drizzle it over tilapia and broccoli, making sure everything is coated evenly.
5. Bake within 20 mins till tilapia flakes easily. Cool it down, then serve.

Nutritional Values: Calories: 240; Carbs: 9g; Fat: 10g; Protein: 31g; Fiber: 3g; Sodium 100mg

32. Cheesy Salmon Frittata

Preparation time: 15 minutes
Cooking time: 10 minutes
Servings: 4

Ingredients:
- Eight big egg whites
- One-fourth cup skim milk
- One-fourth tsp pepper
- One-fourth tsp garlic powder
- One tbsp olive oil
- One red bell pepper, chopped
- One cup chopped baby spinach leaves
- One cup cooked salmon, flaked into pieces
- Three-fourth cup shredded low-fat mozzarella cheese

Directions:
1. Warm up your oven to 375F (190C).
2. In your medium container, whisk egg whites, milk, pepper, plus garlic powder.
3. Warm up olive oil in your ovenproof skillet on moderate temp. Put red bell pepper, then cook within 3 mins till soften.
4. Add the chopped spinach leaves, then cook within one min. Pour egg mixture and distribute the salmon pieces evenly. Sprinkle the shredded low-fat mozzarella cheese on top.
5. Cook within 5 mins on moderate-low temp. Meanwhile, preheat your broiler on high.
6. Place the skillet under the broiler within 2 mins till cheese is slightly golden. Cool it down, then serve.

Nutritional Values: Calories: 245; Carbs: 6g; Fat: 11g; Protein: 31g; Fiber: 1g; Sodium 250mg

33.   Citrus Grilled Shrimp Skewers

Preparation time: 15 minutes + marinating time
Cooking time: 10 minutes
Servings: 4

Ingredients:

- One-pound peeled & deveined shrimp
- Two minced garlic cloves
- Zest of one lemon
- Zest of one lime
- One-fourth cup fresh lemon juice
- One-fourth cup fresh lime juice
- Zest tbsp olive oil
- One tsp honey
- Half tsp black pepper
- One-fourth tsp smoked paprika

Directions:

1. In your small container, whisk garlic, lemon & lime zest, lemon & lime juice, olive oil, honey, black pepper, plus smoked paprika.
2. Put shrimp in your shallow dish, pour marinade, then toss evenly. Cover, then marinate in your fridge within one hour.
3. Warm up your grill on moderate-high temp. Thread the shrimp onto the skewers evenly spaced apart.
4. Grill shrimp skewers within 4-5 mins on each side till opaque. Cool it down, then serve.

Nutritional Values: Calories: 212; Carbs: 6g; Fat: 9g; Protein: 25g; Fiber: 0g; Sodium 134mg

34. Garlic Butter Baked Cod

Preparation time: 10 minutes
Cooking time: 12-15 minutes
Servings: 4

Ingredients:

- Four (six oz each) cod fillets, pat dried
- Two tbsp unsalted butter, melted
- Three garlic cloves, minced
- One tbsp fresh lemon juice
- One tsp dried parsley
- One-fourth tsp black pepper

Directions:

1. Warm up your oven to 400°F (200°C). Line your baking sheet using foil.
2. Put cod fillets onto your baking sheet.
3. In your small container, mix melted unsalted butter, minced garlic, lemon juice, dried parsley, and black pepper. Evenly pour the garlic butter mixture over each cod fillet, making sure to spread it.
4. Bake within 12-15 mins till cod easily flakes. Cool it down, then serve.

Nutritional Values: Calories: 183; Carbs: 2g; Fat: 7g; Protein: 29g; Fiber: 0g; Sodium 110mg

35.   Jamaican Jerk Snapper

Preparation time: 15 minutes + marinating time
Cooking time: 10 minutes
Servings: 4

Ingredients:
- Four (six oz each) snapper fillets
- One tbsp olive oil
- Two tbsp soy sauce, low-sodium
- Two tsp minced garlic
- One tsp grated ginger
- One-fourth cup chopped green onion
- One-fourth cup chopped fresh cilantro
- Half tsp allspice
- Half tsp paprika
- Juice of one lime

Directions:
1. In your small container, whisk oil, soy sauce, garlic, ginger, chopped green onion, chopped cilantro, allspice, paprika, and lime juice.
2. Arrange snapper fillets in your shallow container, then add marinade. Make sure each fillet is well-coated. Marinate within 30 mins in your fridge.
3. Warm up your grill or grill pan to moderate-high temp. Add snapper fillets, then cook within 4 to 5 mins per side, till fish flakes easily. Serve.

Nutritional Values: Calories: 208; Carbs: 3g; Fat: 7g; Protein: 34g; Fiber: 0g; Sodium 270mg

36.   Orange Ginger Glazed Scallops

Preparation time: 10 minutes + marinating time
Cooking time: 9 minutes
Servings: 4

Ingredients:

- One-pound Sea scallops, rinsed and patted dry
- One cup freshly squeezed orange juice
- One-fourth cup soy sauce, low-sodium
- Two tbsp grated ginger, fresh
- One tbsp honey
- Two garlic cloves, minced
- One tsp grated orange zest
- One-fourth tsp black pepper, ground
- Two tbsp olive oil

Directions:

1. In your small container, whisk orange juice, low-sodium soy sauce, grated ginger, honey, minced garlic, orange zest, plus pepper.
2. In your shallow container, place the scallops, pour marinade, then marinate within 30 mins.
3. Warm up olive oil in your big skillet on moderate-high temp. Remove scallops from your marinade, reserving the liquid for later use. Sear the scallops within 2 mins per side till golden.
4. Meanwhile, in your small saucepan on moderate-high temp, let reserved marinade boil, adjust to low temp, then simmer within 5 mins till slightly thickened.
5. Drizzle the thickened glaze over the cooked scallops. Serve.

Nutritional Values: Calories: 210; Carbs: 14g; Fat: 7g; Protein: 23g; Fiber: 1g; Sodium 410mg

37. Almond Crusted Halibut

Preparation time: 15 minutes
Cooking time: 20 minutes
Servings: 4

Ingredients:
- Four (six oz each) Halibut fillets
- One cup almond flour
- Half cup unsalted almonds, finely chopped
- One-fourth cup freshly grated Parmesan cheese (optional)
- Half tsp each of garlic powder & onion powder
- One-fourth tsp black pepper
- Two egg whites, lightly beaten
- Cooking spray or olive oil for greasing

Directions:
1. Warm up your oven to 425°F (220°C).
2. In your shallow container, mix together almond flour, chopped almonds, Parmesan cheese, garlic & onion powder, plus pepper.
3. Dip each Halibut fillet into egg whites, and coat into almond mixture.
4. Oil your baking sheet using cooking spray, then add coated Halibut fillets. Bake within 18-20 mins till fish flakes easily. Serve.

Nutritional Values: Calories: 482; Carbs: 10g; Fat: 33g; Protein: 42g; Fiber: 5g; Sodium 170mg

38. Thai Green Curry Steamed Mussels

Preparation time: 15 minutes

Cooking time: 15 minutes

Servings: 4

Ingredients:

- Two pounds fresh mussels, cleaned & debearded
- One tbsp olive oil
- One small thinly sliced red onion
- Two garlic cloves, minced
- One cup unsweetened coconut milk
- Three tbsp low-sodium Thai green curry paste
- Two tbsp lime juice
- One-fourth cup chopped fresh cilantro

Directions:

1. In your big pot, warm up olive oil on moderate temp. Put red onion, then cook within 5 mins till softened.
2. Put garlic, then cook within one min.
3. Stir in the unsweetened coconut milk and low-sodium Thai green curry paste. Let it simmer.
4. Put cleaned mussels, cover, then steam within 8–10 mins till mussels have opened. Remove the pot from heat and discard any unopened mussels. Mix in lime juice plus cilantro. Serve.

Nutritional Values: Calories: 381; Carbs: 16g; Fat: 22g; Protein: 31g; Fiber: 2g; Sodium 321mg

Poultry Recipes

39. Hot Chicken Wings

Preparation time: 15 minutes
Cooking time: 45 minutes
Servings: 4

Ingredients:
- Two pounds chicken wings, tips removed, and separated at the joint
- One-fourth cup melted unsalted butter
- One-fourth cup hot sauce, low-sodium
- Two garlic cloves, minced
- Half tsp cayenne pepper, ground
- Half tsp smoked paprika
- One-fourth tsp onion powder
- Black pepper, to taste
- Cooking spray (non-stick)

Directions:
1. Warm up your oven to 400°F (200°C). Line your baking sheet using foil, then grease using non-stick cooking spray.
2. In your big container, mix melted butter, hot sauce, garlic, cayenne pepper, smoked paprika, onion powder, plus black pepper. Toss in chicken wings till evenly coated.
3. Arrange coated chicken wings in your baking sheet. Bake within 45 mins till chicken wings are crispy. Cool it down. Serve.

Nutritional Values: Calories: 450; Carbs: 3g; Fat: 34g; Protein: 32g; Fiber: 0g; Sodium 420mg

40.   Spicy Turkey Chili

Preparation time: 15 minutes
Cooking time: 45 minutes
Servings: 6

Ingredients:
- One-pound lean ground turkey
- One tbsp olive oil
- One big chopped onion
- One chopped red bell pepper
- Two minced garlic cloves
- Two (14.5 oz each) cans diced tomatoes, no-salt-added
- One (15 oz) can black beans, no-salt-added, strained & washed
- One (15 oz) can kidney beans, no-salt-added, strained & washed
- Two cups low-sodium vegetable broth
- One tbsp chili powder
- One tbsp cumin, ground
- Half tbsp smoked paprika
- ground black pepper, as required

Directions:
1. In your big pot, warm up olive oil on moderate temp. Put ground turkey, then cook till browned, breaking it up.
2. Put onion, red bell pepper, plus garlic, then cook within 5 mins till vegetables have softened.
3. Mix in diced tomatoes, black & kidney beans, vegetable broth, chili powder, cumin, paprika, plus black pepper.
4. Let it boil, then simmer within 30 mins, stirring occasionally. Taste your chili and adjust seasonings as desired. Serve.

Nutritional Values: Calories: 281; Carbs: 27g; Fat: 9g; Protein: 23g; Fiber: 8g; Sodium 225mg

41.   Oven-Baked Pesto Chicken

Preparation time: 15 minutes
Cooking time: 25 minutes
Servings: 4

Ingredients:

- Four no bones & skin chicken breasts, washed & pat dried
- Half cup low-sodium pesto sauce
- One-third cup low-sodium mozzarella cheese, shredded
- Half cup cherry tomatoes, halved
- One tbsp olive oil

Directions:

1. Warm up your oven to 400°F (200°C).
2. Grease your baking dish using olive oil, then add chicken breasts in it. Spread a generous layer of low-sodium pesto sauce on each chicken breast.
3. Scatter the halved cherry tomatoes around and over the chicken breasts. Sprinkle with the low-sodium mozzarella cheese evenly. Bake within 25 mins till cheese is golden. Cool it down, then serve.

Nutritional Values: Calories: 355; Carbs: 7g; Fat: 18g; Protein: 42g; Fiber: 1g; Sodium 200mg

42. Greek Turkey Feta Burger

Preparation time: 15 minutes
Cooking time: 11 minutes
Servings: 4

Ingredients:

- One-pound lean ground turkey
- One-fourth cup finely chopped red onion
- One-third cup crumbled feta cheese
- One-fourth cup kalamata olives, chopped
- Two tbsp chopped fresh parsley
- One tsp dried oregano
- One-fourth tsp black pepper
- Cooking spray or olive oil
- 4 whole-grain burger buns

Directions:

1. In your container, mix ground turkey, red onion, feta, kalamata olives, parsley, oregano, plus pepper. Form the mixture into four equal-sized patties.
2. Warm up your grill or grill pan on moderate temp, then grease using olive oil. Grill patties within 5 mins on each side till cooked through.
3. Toast the burger buns on the grill for about 1 minute or until slightly browned. Assemble the burgers by placing a patty on each of the toasted buns' bottom halves. Close it using half of bun on each burger. Serve.

Nutritional Values: Calories: 410; Carbs: 35g; Fat: 16g; Protein: 35g; Fiber: 5g; Sodium 410mg

43.   Paprika Chicken Over Cauliflower Rice

Preparation time: 15 minutes
Cooking time: 28 minutes
Servings: 4

Ingredients:

- Four no bones & skin chicken breasts
- One tbsp olive oil
- One tsp smoked paprika
- Half tsp each of garlic powder, onion powder & oregano, dried
- One-fourth tsp black pepper
- One medium head cauliflower, grated
- One cup diced each of red bell pepper & zucchini
- One cup cherry tomato, halved
- Two cups baby spinach leaves

Directions:
Warm up your oven to 400°F (200°C).

1. In your small container, mix paprika, garlic & onion powder, dried oregano, plus pepper. Rub it evenly over both sides of chicken breasts.
2. Warm up olive oil in your big oven-safe skillet on moderate-high temp.
3. Sear seasoned chicken breasts within 2 mins on each side till golden. Remove, then put aside.
4. Put cauliflower rice to your skillet, then cook within 3 mins till slightly tender. Mix in bell peppers, zucchini, plus cherry tomatoes. Cook within 3 mins. Nestle chicken breasts among vegetables.
5. Transfer skillet to your oven, then bake within 20 mins till chicken is golden. Remove, then mix in fresh baby spinach leaves until they wilt slightly.

Nutritional Values: Calories: 321; Carbs: 14g; Fat: 10g; Protein: 40g; Fiber: 5g; Sodium 170mg

44.   Tex-Mex Turkey Burrito Bowls

Preparation time: 20 minutes
Cooking time: 30 minutes
Servings: 4

Ingredients:
- One-pound lean ground turkey
- One cup brown rice, uncooked
- Two cups chicken broth, low-sodium
- Half cup low-sodium black beans, washed & strained
- One-fourth cup chopped cilantro
- Two cups frozen corn, thawed
- Two cup cherry tomatoes, halved
- Two avocados, diced
- One-fourth cup chopped green onions
- One tbsp olive oil
- Two tsp low-sodium taco seasoning
- One-fourth tsp cumin, ground
- One-fourth tsp chili powder

Directions:
1. In your medium saucepan, mix brown rice plus broth. Let it boil, adjust to low temp, cover then simmer within 25-30 mins till rice is fully cooked. Remove, then let it stand within 5 mins before fluffing.
2. While the rice cooks, warm up your skillet with olive oil on moderate temp. Put ground turkey, breaking it up into small pieces till browned. Mix in low-sodium taco seasoning, cumin, and chili powder.
3. To assemble burrito bowls, divide cooked brown rice among four serving bowls. Top the rice with cooked turkey mixture, black beans, corn, cherry tomatoes, avocado, and green onions. Serve.

Nutritional Values: Calories: 520; Carbs: 57g; Fat: 18g; Protein: 39g; Fiber: 11g; Sodium 250mg

45.   Baked Chicken Breast with Cherry Tomatoes

Preparation time: 15 minutes
Cooking time: 31 minutes
Servings: 4

Ingredients:

- Four no bones & skin chicken breasts
- One tbsp olive oil
- Two cups cherry tomatoes, halved
- Half cup low-sodium chicken broth
- One-fourth cup fresh basil, chopped
- Two garlic cloves, minced
- Salt & pepper, as required

Directions:

1. Warm up your oven to 375°F (190°C). Flavor chicken breasts using salt plus pepper.
2. In your big oven-safe skillet, warm up olive oil on moderate temp. Add chicken breasts, then cook within 3 mins on each side till golden. Remove the chicken, then put aside.
3. Add garlic to your skillet, then cook within a min till fragrant. Add cherry tomatoes and broth, then let it boil. Adjust to a simmer, then cook within 5 mins, stirring occasionally. Stir in half of the chopped basil, then add chicken breasts.
4. Transfer skillet to your oven, then bake within 18-20 mins till chicken is cooked through. Serve.

Nutritional Values: Calories: 210; Carbs: 7g; Fat: 6g; Protein: 31g; Fiber: 1g; Sodium 170mg

46. Turkey White Bean Chili

Preparation time: 15 minutes
Cooking time: 35 minutes
Servings: 6

Ingredients:

- One-pound ground turkey, lean
- Two tbsp olive oil
- One big chopped onion
- Two minced garlic cloves
- Two (15 oz) cans white beans, no-salt-added, strained & washed
- Four cups chicken broth, low-sodium
- One green bell pepper, diced
- Two tsp ground cumin
- One tsp dried oregano
- One-fourth tsp black pepper

Directions:

1. In your big pot, warm up olive oil on moderate temp. Put ground turkey, then cook till browned, crumbling it up.
2. Add onion plus garlic, then cook within 5 mins till softened.
3. Mix in white beans, chicken broth, green bell pepper, ground cumin, dried oregano, plus black pepper. Let it boil.
4. Adjust to a simmer within 30-40 mins till cooked. Serve.

Nutritional Values: Calories: 325; Carbs: 38g; Fat: 10g; Protein: 28g; Fiber: 10g; Sodium 180mg

Red Meat Recipes

47.   Greek Lamb Meatballs

Preparation time: 15 minutes
Cooking time: 25 minutes
Servings: 4

Ingredients:
- One-pound lean ground lamb
- One-fourth cup whole wheat breadcrumbs
- One-fourth cup chopped fresh parsley
- Two garlic cloves, minced
- One small red onion, finely chopped
- One-fourth cup crumbled feta cheese
- One tsp dried oregano
- Half tsp each of ground cumin & black pepper
- Non-stick cooking spray

Directions:
1. Warm up your oven to 375°F (190°C). Line your baking sheet using foil, then grease with non-stick cooking spray.
2. In your big container, combine the ground lamb, breadcrumbs, parsley, garlic, red onion, feta, oregano, cumin, plus pepper.
3. Shape the mixture into approximately 16 small meatballs, then place them on your baking sheet. Bake within 25 to 30 mins till meatballs are browned on the outside. Serve.

Nutritional Values: Calories: 280; Carbs: 9g; Fat: 16g; Protein: 24g; Fiber: 1g; Sodium 140mg

48. Garlic and Rosemary Beef Kabobs

Preparation time: 15 minutes + marinating time
Cooking time: 10 minutes
Servings: 4

Ingredients:

- One-pound lean beef sirloin, sliced into one" cubes
- Four minced garlic cloves
- Two tbsp fresh chopped rosemary
- Two tbsp olive oil
- One-fourth tsp black pepper
- Sixteen cherry tomatoes
- One big each of green & red bell pepper, sliced into one" pieces

Directions:

1. In your big container, mix beef cubes with minced garlic, rosemary, olive oil, and black pepper. Toss until evenly coated. Cover, then marinate in your fridge within 30 mins.
2. Warm up your grill or grill pan to moderate-high temp. Assemble skewers by alternating marinated beef cubes with cherry tomatoes and bell pepper pieces.
3. Grill the kabobs for about 10 minutes or until the desired level of doneness is reached, turning occasionally for even cooking. Serve.

Nutritional Values: Calories: 315; Carbs: 8g; Fat: 17g; Protein: 34g; Fiber: 2g; Sodium 95mg

49.   Orange Pork Tenderloin

Preparation time: 15 minutes + marinating time
Cooking time: 30 minutes
Servings: 4

Ingredients:
- One-pound trimmed pork tenderloin
- Three-fourth cup fresh orange juice
- Two tbsp soy sauce, low-sodium
- Two tbsp honey
- Two minced garlic cloves
- One tsp grated ginger, fresh
- One-fourth tsp black pepper, ground
- One tbsp olive oil

Directions:
1. In your big container, whisk orange juice, low-sodium soy sauce, honey, garlic, ginger plus black pepper until well combined.
2. Add pork tenderloin, mix well, cover, then marinate in your fridge within 2 hours, turning occasionally.
3. Warm up your oven to 400°F (200°C). Remove pork, then and reserve the marinade for later.
4. In your ovenproof skillet, warm up olive oil on moderate-high temp, sear pork till browned on all sides.
5. Transfer skillet to your oven, then roast within 20 mins till cooked.
6. Meanwhile, pour reserved marinade into your small saucepan, let it boil, then simmer within 5 minutes to reduce.
7. Remove the pork, let it rest within 5 mins before slicing it into medallions of desired thickness.
8. Drizzle reduced marinade over sliced tenderloin before serving.

Nutritional Values: Calories: 279; Carbs: 20g; Fat: 9g; Protein: 31g; Fiber: 0g; Sodium 281mg

50. Balsamic-Glazed Lamb Chops

Preparation time: 15 minutes

Cooking time: 12 minutes

Servings: 4

Ingredients:

- Eight lamb chops, trimmed of excess fat
- Salt-free seasoning blend (such as Mrs. Dash) to taste
- One-fourth cup balsamic vinegar
- Two tbsp honey
- Two tbsp olive oil
- Two minced garlic cloves
- ground black pepper, as required

Directions:

1. Flavor lamb chops on both sides using seasoning salt-free blend.
2. In your small container, whisk balsamic vinegar and honey until well combined. Put aside.
3. Warm up your olive oil in your big skillet on moderate temp. Put minced garlic, then cook within a min till fragrant.
4. Add lamb chops, then cook within 4 mins per side till browned. Remove lamb chops from the skillet and transfer to your plate; cover it slightly using foil.
5. Return your skillet to moderate temp, then heat pour balsamic-honey mixture. Cook within 3-4 mins till thickens slightly.
6. Return lamb chops back to the skillet, turning them over in the glaze to coat fully. Serve.

Nutritional Values: Calories: 356; Carbs: 12g; Fat: 22g; Protein: 26g; Fiber: 0g; Sodium 90mg

51.   Herb-Crusted Sirloin Tip Roast

Preparation time: 15 minutes
Cooking time: 1 hour & 30 minutes
Servings: 6

Ingredients:
- Three pounds sirloin tip roast
- Two tbsp olive oil
- Three garlic cloves, minced
- One tbsp each of fresh chopped rosemary, thyme & parsley
- Half tsp black pepper, ground
- One-fourth tsp paprika

Directions:
1. Warm up your oven to 325°F (160°C).
2. In your small container, mix minced garlic, chopped rosemary, thyme, parsley, ground black pepper, plus paprika.
3. Rub sirloin tip roast all over using olive oil. Press the herb mixture onto the surface of the roast.
4. Put roast on your rack in your roasting pan.
5. Cook within 1 hour and 30 mins till it cooked through. Adjust cooking time to achieve desired doneness. Cool it down, slice, then serve.

Nutritional Values: Calories: 460; Carbs: 1g; Fat: 28g; Protein: 49g; Fiber: 1g; Sodium 120mg

52.　Apricot-Stuffed Pork Loin

Preparation time: 20 minutes

Cooking time: 50 minutes

Servings: 6

Ingredients:

- Two pounds boneless pork loin
- One cup chopped & dried apricots
- One-fourth cup fresh parsley, minced
- Two minced garlic cloves
- One-fourth tsp each of ground black pepper, dried thyme & dried rosemary
- Three tbsp olive oil
- Half cup chicken broth, low-sodium

Directions:

1. Warm up your oven to 375°F (190°C).
2. Butterfly the pork loin to make a large, flat surface.
3. In your small container, mix chopped apricots, minced parsley, minced garlic, ground black pepper, dried thyme, and dried rosemary.
4. Spread the filling evenly over the opened pork loin. Carefully roll up the pork loin tightly and secure with kitchen twine or toothpicks.
5. Warm up olive oil in your big ovenproof skillet on moderate-high temp. Sear stuffed pork loin till nicely browned.
6. Remove, then pour broth around pork loin.
7. Transfer skillet to your oven, then cook within 45 mins till 145°F (63°C) is reached. Cool it down. Slice, then serve.

Nutritional Values: Calories: 410; Carbs: 16g; Fat: 25g; Protein: 31g; Fiber: 2g; Sodium 100mg

53. Moroccan-Spiced Lamb Skewers

Preparation time: 15 minutes + marinating time
Cooking time: 10-15 minutes
Servings: 4

Ingredients:

- One-pound lean lamb, sliced into one" cubes
- Three tbsp olive oil
- Two minced garlic cloves
- One tsp each of ground cumin & coriander
- Half tsp ground cinnamon
- One-fourth tsp low-sodium ground paprika
- One-fourth tsp ground ginger
- One-fourth tsp black pepper

Directions:

1. In your big container, whisk olive oil, garlic, cumin, coriander, cinnamon, paprika, ginger plus black pepper.
2. Add lamb cubes, then coat it well. Cover, then marinate within one hour in your fridge.
3. Warm up your grill to moderate-high temp.
4. Thread marinated lamb chunks onto your skewers, leaving a small gap between each piece to ensure even cooking.
5. Grill the skewers within 10-15 mins, turning often till cooked. Serve.

Nutritional Values: Calories: 325; Carbs: 3g; Fat: 20g; Protein: 30g; Fiber: 1g; Sodium 90mg

54. Soy-Ginger Marinated Flank Steak

Preparation time: 15 minutes + marinating time

Cooking time: 15 minutes

Servings: 4

Ingredients:

- One-pound flank steak
- One-fourth cup low-sodium soy sauce
- Two tbsp rice vinegar
- One tbsp fresh grated ginger
- Two minced garlic cloves
- One tbsp brown sugar
- One tbsp sesame oil
- One-fourth tsp black pepper

Directions:

1. In your big shallow container, mix low-sodium soy sauce, rice vinegar, ginger, garlic, sugar, oil, plus pepper. Mix in flank steak, then marinate in your fridge within 2 hours.
2. Warm up your grill on moderate-high temp. Grill marinated flank steak within 6-7 mins per side till cooked through.
3. Remove the steak, then let it rest within 5 mins before slicing against the grain. Serve.

Nutritional Values: Calories: 320; Carbs: 8g; Fat: 18g; Protein: 30g; Fiber: 0g; Sodium 550mg

Vegetables Recipes

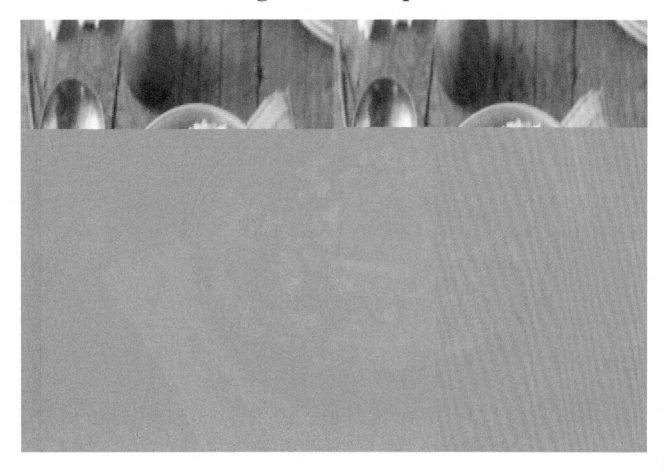

55. Butternut Squash Lentil Quinoa Gratin

Preparation time: 20 minutes
Cooking time: 45 minutes
Servings: 6

Ingredients:

- One medium butternut squash, peeled & cubed
- One cup uncooked quinoa
- One cup green lentil, washed & strained
- Four cups vegetable broth, low-sodium
- One medium chopped onion
- Three minced garlic cloves
- One tbsp olive oil
- Two cups chopped baby spinach
- One tsp dried thyme
- Half tsp black pepper
- Three-fourth cup shredded low-sodium mozzarella cheese

Directions:

1. Warm up your oven to 375°F (190°C).
2. In your big skillet, warm up olive oil on moderate-high temp. Put onion plus garlic, then cook within 5 mins till softened.
3. Put butternut squash, lentils, quinoa, vegetable broth, thyme, plus pepper. Let it boil, then simmer within 20 mins till quinoa is cooked through. Stir in chopped spinach until wilted.
4. Transfer it into your big greased baking dish. Sprinkle evenly with low-sodium mozzarella cheese. Bake within 20 mins till cheese is melted. Cool it down. Serve.

Nutritional Values: Calories: 330; Carbs: 54g; Fat: 7g; Protein: 16g; Fiber: 12g; Sodium 180mg

56.   Cauliflower Fried Rice

Preparation time: 10 minutes
Cooking time: 20 minutes
Servings: 4

Ingredients:
- Four cups cauliflower rice
- One tbsp olive oil
- One small onion, diced
- Two garlic minced cloves
- One cup frozen mixed vegetable (peas, carrots, corn)
- Two big eggs, beaten
- One-fourth cup low-sodium soy sauce
- Three chopped green onions
- One tsp sesame oil
- ground black pepper, as required

Directions:
1. Warm up olive oil in your big skillet on moderate-high temp. Add onion plus garlic, then sauté within 5 mins till fragrant.
2. Mix in frozen mixed vegetables and cook within 5 minutes till warmed through.
3. Push them to one side of your skillet, then pour eggs on empty side. Scramble it till cooked through.
4. Add cauliflower rice, mixing everything together. Pour low-sodium soy sauce over the cauliflower rice mixture and stir well to incorporate.
5. Cook within 5 mins, allowing flavors to meld together. Remove, then mix in green onions, sesame oil, plus black pepper. Serve.

Nutritional Values: Calories: 205; Carbs: 20g; Fat: 9g; Protein: 11g; Fiber: 6g; Sodium 300mg

57. Ginger Soy Bok Choy Stir-Fry

Preparation time: 15 minutes
Cooking time: 8 minutes
Servings: 4

Ingredients:

- One-pound bok choy, washed and chopped
- One tbsp soy sauce, low-sodium
- One tbsp rice vinegar
- Two tsp sesame oil
- Two tsp grated fresh ginger
- Two minced garlic cloves
- Half cup each of onion & red bell pepper, thinly sliced
- Half cup thinly sliced onion
- One tbsp olive oil

Directions:

1. In your small container, whisk soy sauce, rice vinegar, oil, plus grated fresh ginger. Put aside.
2. Warm up olive oil in your big skillet on moderate temp. Put garlic, then cook within 30 seconds till fragrant.
3. Add red bell pepper plus onion, then cook within 3 mins, mixing often. Mix in chopped bok choy, then cook within 3 mins till tender. Pour ginger soy sauce mixture, then toss well.
4. Cook for another minute or so to let flavors meld together. Serve.

Nutritional Values: Calories: 120; Carbs: 10g; Fat: 7g; Protein: 4g; Fiber: 3g; Sodium 200mg

58.   Baked Zucchini Boats with Lentils

Preparation time: 15 minutes
Cooking time: 45 minutes
Servings: 4

Ingredients:
- Four medium halved zucchini
- One cup cooked lentil
- One cup no-sodium diced tomatoes
- One cup low-sodium vegetable broth
- Half cup each of red bell pepper & onion, chopped
- Two minced garlic cloves
- Two tbsp olive oil
- One tbsp chopped fresh parsley
- One tsp dried oregano
- One-fourth tsp black pepper

Directions:
1. Warm up your oven to 375°F (190°C).
2. Scoop out flesh of zucchini halves, leaving a shell around one-fourth" thick. Reserve scooped flesh for later use.
3. In your big skillet, warm up olive oil on moderate temp.
4. Put onion plus red bell pepper, then cook within 4 mins till softened. Mix in garlic, then cook within another min.
5. Put reserved zucchini flesh, diced tomatoes, cooked lentils, vegetable broth, parsley, oregano, plus pepper. Cook within 5 mins.
6. Using a spoon, divide lentil mixture evenly on your zucchini boats. Put filled zucchini boats into your baking dish, then cover using foil. Bake within 30 mins till zucchini is tender. Serve.

Nutritional Values: Calories: 200; Carbs: 29g; Fat: 7g; Protein: 12g; Fiber: 9g; Sodium 170mg

59. Grilled Portobello Mushrooms

Preparation time: 15 minutes + marinating time
Cooking time: 10 minutes
Servings: 4

Ingredients:

- Four big Portobello mushrooms, stems and gills removed
- Two tbsp olive oil
- Two tbsp lemon juice, freshly squeezed
- One tbsp low-sodium soy sauce
- One minced garlic clove
- One tsp each of dried basil & oregano
- Half tsp ground black pepper

Directions:

1. In your small container, whisk olive oil, soy sauce, lemon juice, garlic, basil, oregano, plus black pepper to create the marinade.
2. Put Portobello mushrooms in your shallow container, then pour marinade. Ensure that mushrooms are well-coated by turning them over a few times. Cover the dish, then marinate in your fridge within 30 mins.
3. Warm up grill to moderate-high temp.
4. Once heated, place the marinated mushrooms on the grill with the gill side up. Cook within 5 mins till slightly soften.
5. Flip mushrooms over, then continue grilling within 5 mins till tender. Serve.

Nutritional Values: Calories: 95; Carbs: 4g; Fat: 7g; Protein: 3g; Fiber: 1g; Sodium 182mg

60.   Chickpea and Vegetable Curry

Preparation time: 15 minutes
Cooking time: 30 minutes
Servings: 4

Ingredients:
- One tbsp olive oil
- One big chopped onion
- Two minced garlic cloves
- One tbsp low-sodium curry powder
- One tsp ground cumin
- Half tsp turmeric
- One (15 oz) can low-sodium chickpeas, strained & washed
- One cup vegetable broth, low-sodium
- Two cups assorted vegetables (e.g., bell peppers, zucchini, carrots), chopped
- One (14.5 oz) can diced tomatoes, no-salt-added & undrained
- Three cups cooked brown rice, for serving

Directions:
1. Warm up your olive oil in your big skillet on moderate temp. Put onion plus garlic, then cook within 5 mins till softened.
2. Mix in curry powder, ground cumin, plus turmeric. Cook within another min till fragrant. Put chickpeas, vegetable broth, assorted vegetables, and diced tomatoes plus its juice. Let it boil.
3. Adjust to low temp, then simmer within 20 mins till vegetables are tender. Serve the curry over brown rice.

Nutritional Values: Calories: 385; Carbs: 68g; Fat: 7g; Protein: 14g; Fiber: 11g; Sodium 240mg

61. Caramelized Brussels Sprouts

Preparation time: 15 minutes
Cooking time: 23 minutes
Servings: 4

Ingredients:

- One-pound Brussels sprouts, halved
- Three tbsp olive oil, divided
- One-fourth tsp ground black pepper
- Two minced garlic cloves
- One tbsp balsamic vinegar
- One tbsp honey or maple syrup
- One-fourth cup low-sodium vegetable broth

Directions:

1. Warm up your oven to 400°F (200°C).
2. In your big container, mix Brussels sprouts, two tbsp olive oil, plus pepper.
3. Transfer the sprouts onto your baking sheet, then roast within 20-25 mins till tender and slightly caramelized, stirring once time.
4. Meanwhile, heat the remaining oil in your small saucepan on moderate temp. Put minced garlic, then cook within one min till fragrant.
5. Mix in balsamic vinegar, honey or maple syrup, and low-sodium vegetable broth. Simmer within 3 mins till thickened slightly.
6. Remove roasted Brussels sprouts, then transfer them to your serving dish. Drizzle balsamic glaze over sprouts, then toss well. Serve.

Nutritional Values: Calories: 165; Carbs: 17g; Fat: 10g; Protein: 4g; Fiber: 4g; Sodium 55mg

62.   Roasted Cauliflower Steak

Preparation time: 15 minutes
Cooking time: 30 minutes
Servings: 4

Ingredients:
- One big head cauliflower, trimmed and sliced into 3/4-inch-thick steaks
- Three tbsp olive oil
- One tsp each of garlic powder & onion powder
- Half tsp smoked paprika
- One-fourth tsp ground black pepper
- Two tbsp fresh lemon juice

Directions:
1. Warm up your oven to 400°F (200°C).
2. In your small container, mix garlic powder, onion powder, smoked paprika, plus pepper.
3. Put cauliflower steaks on your baking sheet lined using parchment paper. Brush cauliflower steak using olive oil.
4. Flavor it with seasoning mix evenly over both sides of the cauliflower steaks.
5. Roast the cauliflower steaks in your oven within 15 mins, flip, then cook within 15 mins till tender.
6. Drizzle lemon juice over roasted cauliflower steaks. Serve.

Nutritional Values: Calories: 173; Carbs: 11g; Fat: 14g; Protein: 4g; Fiber: 5g; Sodium 58mg

Soups Recipes

63.   Ground Beef and Mixed Vegetable Soup

Preparation time: 15 minutes
Cooking time: 38 minutes
Servings: 6

Ingredients:
- One-pound lean ground beef
- Four cups low-sodium beef broth
- One medium onion, chopped
- Two minced garlic cloves
- Three cups mixed vegetables
- One (14.5 oz) can diced tomatoes, no-sodium & unstrained
- One tbsp low-sodium Worcestershire sauce
- One tsp oregano, dried
- Half tsp black pepper

Directions:
1. In your big pot, cook ground beef within 5 mins on moderate temp till browned, breaking it into crumbles as you cook. Strain.
2. Put onion plus garlic, then cook within 3-4 mins till onion is tender.
3. Mix in mixed vegetables, beef broth, diced tomatoes (with their juice), Worcestershire sauce, oregano, and black pepper.
4. Let it boil on high temp, adjust to low temp and simmer within 30-35 mins till vegetables are tender. Serve.

Nutritional Values: Calories: 210; Carbs: 21g; Fat: 6g; Protein: 20g; Fiber: 4g; Sodium 250mg

64. Tomato Basil Soup

Preparation time: 10 minutes
Cooking time: 35 minutes
Servings: 6

Ingredients:
- Two tbsp olive oil
- One medium onion, chopped
- Two minced garlic cloves
- Four cups low-sodium vegetable broth
- Two (28 oz) cans no-salt-added crushed tomatoes
- One-fourth cup fresh basil leaves, chopped
- One-fourth tsp ground black pepper
- One-fourth tsp paprika

Directions:
1. In your big pot, warm up olive oil on moderate temp. Put chopped onion, then cook within 5 mins till softened. Put minced garlic, then cook within one min.
2. Stir in the low-sodium vegetable broth, no-salt-added crushed tomatoes, chopped basil, ground black pepper, and paprika.
3. Let it boil, adjust to low temp, then simmer within 30 mins. Blend using immersion blender till smooth. Serve.

Nutritional Values: Calories: 129; Carbs: 19g; Fat: 4g; Protein: 3g; Fiber: 4g; Sodium 290mg

65. Lemon Chicken Orzo Soup

Preparation time: 15 minutes
Cooking time: 30 minutes
Servings: 6

Ingredients:
- One tbsp olive oil
- One medium chopped onion
- Two minced garlic cloves
- Six cups chicken broth, no-sodium-added
- Two no bones & skin chicken breasts, cooked and shredded
- One cup uncooked orzo pasta
- Three cups chopped fresh spinach
- Juice & two lemons
- Salt and pepper, as required

Directions:
1. Warm up olive oil in your big pot on moderate temp.
2. Put onion plus garlic, then cook within 5 mins, stirring occasionally, till onion is tender. Mix in broth, then let it boil. Add shredded chicken plus uncooked orzo pasta.
3. Adjust to moderate-low temp, then simmer within 15-20 mins till orzo is cooked through. Stir in spinach, lemon juice, salt, plus pepper. Simmer within 5 mins till spinach has wilted. Serve hot.

Nutritional Values: Calories: 215; Carbs: 26g; Fat: 5g; Protein: 17g; Fiber: 2g; Sodium 95mg

66. Cauliflower and Broccoli Cheese Soup

Preparation time: 15 minutes
Cooking time: 18 minutes
Servings: 6

Ingredients:

- One medium head cauliflower, sliced into florets
- One medium head broccoli, sliced into florets
- One tbsp olive oil
- One small onion, diced
- Two minced garlic cloves
- Four cups vegetable broth, low-sodium
- Two cups unsweetened almond milk
- One tsp Dijon mustard
- One-fourth tsp nutmeg
- One-fourth tsp black pepper
- One & half cups shredded cheddar cheese, low-sodium

Directions:

1. In your big pot, warm up olive oil on moderate temp. Put onion plus garlic, then cook within 3-4 mins till slightly soften.
2. Mix in cauliflower and broccoli florets, then pour in the low-sodium vegetable broth. Let it boil. Adjust to a simmer, cover, then cook within 15 mins till vegetables are tender.
3. Blend soup using your immersion blender till smooth. If you prefer a chunkier texture, only partially blend the soup.
4. Mix in almond milk, mustard, nutmeg, plus pepper. Allow the soup to heat through. Gradually mix in shredded cheddar till fully combined and melted.
5. Serve hot with whole-grain bread or crackers on the side.

Nutritional Values: Calories: 230; Carbs: 14g; Fat: 14g; Protein: 12g; Fiber: 5g; Sodium 220mg

67.　Red Lentil Creamy Soup

Preparation time: 15 minutes
Cooking time: 30 minutes
Servings: 4-6

Ingredients:
- One cup red lentil, washed & strained
- Four cups vegetable broth, low-sodium
- One medium chopped onion
- Two chopped medium carrots
- Two minced garlic cloves
- One tbsp olive oil
- One tsp cumin, ground
- Half tsp ground turmeric
- Half tsp smoked paprika
- One-fourth tsp black pepper, ground

Directions:
1. Warm up olive oil in your big pot on moderate temp. Put onions plus carrots, then cook within 5 mins till softened.
2. Mix in garlic, cumin, turmeric, smoked paprika, plus pepper, then cook within another min.
3. Add rinsed red lentils and low-sodium vegetable broth to the pot. Let it boil, cover, then simmer within 25 mins till lentils are soft.
4. Puree soup using your immersion blender till creamy. Serve.

Nutritional Values: Calories: 220; Carbs: 34g; Fat: 5g; Protein: 14g; Fiber: 7g; Sodium 150mg

68.   Leek Sweet Potato Soup

Preparation time: 15 minutes

Cooking time: 35 minutes

Servings: 4

Ingredients:

- One tbsp olive oil
- Two medium sweet potatoes, peeled and diced
- Two leeks, washed well and thinly sliced
- Four cups low-sodium vegetable broth
- One tsp dried thyme
- One bay leaf

Directions:
1. Warm up olive oil in your big pot on moderate temp.
2. Put diced sweet potatoes and sliced leeks, then cook within 5 mins till slightly tender, stirring occasionally.
3. Mix in broth, dried thyme, plus bay leaf.
4. Let it boil, adjust to low temp, then simmer within 30-40 mins till sweet potatoes are tender. Discard bay leaf.
5. Blend it using your immersion blender till creamy. Serve.

Nutritional Values: Calories: 166; Carbs: 31g; Fat: 44g; Protein: 3g; Fiber: 4g; Sodium 170mg

69. Asian Mushroom Soup

Preparation time: 15 minutes
Cooking time: 20 minutes
Servings: 4

Ingredients:
- Eight oz mixed Asian mushrooms (shiitake, maitake, enoki), sliced
- One tbsp olive oil
- Four cups low-sodium vegetable broth
- Two cups sliced bok choy
- One tbsp soy sauce, low-sodium
- One tsp grated ginger, fresh
- Two minced garlic cloves
- One-fourth cup chopped green onions
- One-fourth cup fresh chopped cilantro
- Juice of one lime

Directions:
1. Warm up olive oil in your big saucepan on moderate temp.
2. Put mushrooms, then cook within 5 mins till tender, mixing occasionally. Add broth, bok choy, soy sauce, ginger, and minced garlic to the saucepan with the mushrooms.
3. Let it boil, then let simmer within 15 mins till flavors meld. Mix in chopped green onions, cilantro, and lime juice. Serve.

Nutritional Values: Calories: 90; Carbs: 11g; Fat: 4g; Protein: 4g; Fiber: 2g; Sodium 180mg

70.   Cannellini Bean Couscous Soup

Preparation time: 15 minutes
Cooking time: 30 minutes
Servings: 6

Ingredients:

- One tbsp olive oil
- One medium chopped onion
- Two minced garlic cloves
- Two medium diced carrots
- Two celery stalks, diced
- One cup canned cannellini beans, no-salt, washed & strained
- Five cups vegetable broth, low-sodium
- One tsp basil, dried
- Half tsp oregano, dried
- One-fourth tsp black pepper
- One cup whole-wheat couscous
- Six cups baby spinach leaves
- Juice of half a lemon

Directions:

1. In your big pot, warm up olive oil on moderate temp. Add onion plus garlic, then cook within 5 mins till softened.
2. Put carrots plus celery, then cook within 5 mins till slightly soften. Stir in cannellini beans, broth, basil, oregano, plus black pepper. Let it boil. Adjust to low temp, then simmer within 15 mins.
3. Adjust to medium temp and stir in the couscous. Cook within 6 mins till couscous is tender. Mix in spinach, then cook within one min till spinach has wilted.
4. Squeeze the lemon juice into the soup and remove from heat. Serve.

Nutritional Values: Calories: 180; Carbs: 31g; Fat: 4g; Protein: 8g; Fiber: 7g; Sodium 180mg

Salad Recipes

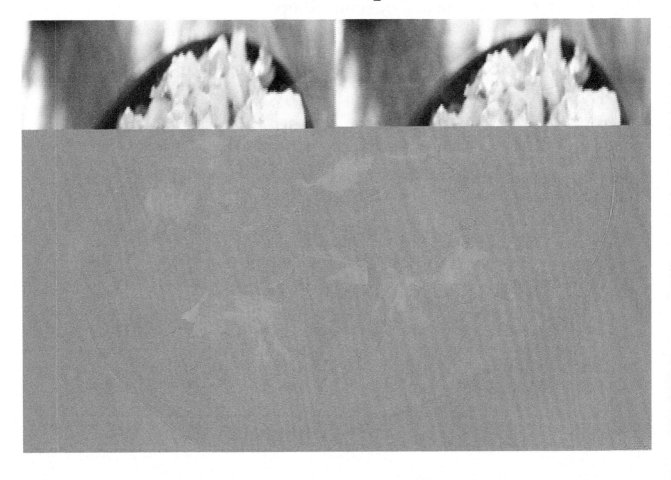

71.   Roasted Cauliflower Salad

Preparation time: 15 minutes
Cooking time: 25 minutes
Servings: 4

Ingredients:
- One big head cauliflower, sliced into florets
- Two tbsp olive oil
- One-fourth tsp black pepper
- Half tsp ground cumin
- Four cups mixed greens
- One-fourth cup sliced red onion
- One-third cup walnuts, chopped & toasted
- One-fourth cup dried cranberries
- Two tbsp red wine vinegar
- Two tbsp olive oil, extra-virgin
- ground black pepper, as required

Directions:
1. Warm up your oven to 425°F (220°C).
2. In your big container, mix cauliflower, olive oil, pepper, plus cumin till coated.
3. Spread it on your parchment-lined baking sheet, then roast within25 mins till tender. Cool it down.
4. In your big separate container, toss mixed greens, red onion, walnuts, plus cranberries. Mix vinegar plus olive oil in your small container.
5. Top salad with roasted cauliflower, then drizzle dressing over top. Toss gently to combine all ingredients. Serve immediately.

Nutritional Values: Calories: 286; Carbs: 18g; Fat: 22g; Protein: 7g; Fiber: 6g; Sodium 100mg

72.   Spinach and Strawberry Salad

Preparation time: 15 minutes
Cooking time: 0 minutes
Servings: 4

Ingredients:
- Four cups fresh baby spinach
- Two cups sliced strawberries
- One-fourth cup crumbled feta cheese (optional, for low-sodium choose a low-sodium variant)
- One-fourth cup chopped walnuts
- One tbsp olive oil, extra virgin
- Two tbsp balsamic vinegar
- One tbsp honey
- Black pepper, as required

Directions:
1. In your big container, combine spinach, strawberries, feta (if using), and chopped walnuts.
2. In your small container, whisk olive oil, balsamic vinegar, honey, plus pepper. Drizzle it over salad, then mix well. Serve.

Nutritional Values: Calories: 220; Carbs: 18g; Fat: 14g; Protein: 5g; Fiber: 4g; Sodium 150mg

73. Greek Quinoa Salad

Preparation time: 20 minutes
Cooking time: 15 minutes
Servings: 4

Ingredients:

- One cup uncooked quinoa
- Two cups water
- One cucumber, diced
- One cup cherry tomato, halved
- One-fourth cup red onion, chopped
- One-fourth cup black olives, pitted and sliced (low-sodium variety)
- One-fourth cup chopped parsley, fresh
- One-fourth cup chopped dill, fresh
- One tbsp olive oil
- Juice of one lemon
- One tsp black pepper
- Optional: crumbled feta cheese (choose a low-sodium brand)

Directions:

1. In your saucepan, boil quinoa plus water, adjust to low temp, cover then simmer within 15 mins till quinoa is cooked.
2. In your big container, mix quinoa, cucumber, tomatoes, onion, black olives, parsley, plus dill.
3. In your small container, whisk olive oil and lemon juice. Pour it on quinoa mixture, then toss well. Flavor it with black pepper.
4. You can add crumbled feta cheese if desired, then chill it in your fridge within one hour. Serve.

Nutritional Values: Calories: 250; Carbs: 34g; Fat: 10g; Protein: 7g; Fiber: 5g; Sodium 70mg

74. Asian Broccoli Slaw Salad

Preparation time: 15 minutes
Cooking time: 0 minutes
Servings: 4

Ingredients:

- Four cups pre-packaged broccoli slaw mix
- One-third cup unsalted cashew nuts, roughly chopped
- One-third cup unsweetened dried cranberries
- One-fourth cup sliced green onions
- Half cup cilantro, chopped
- Two tbsp soy sauce, low-sodium
- Two tbsp rice vinegar
- One tbsp sesame oil
- One tbsp ginger, fresh, minced
- One clove garlic, minced
- Zest & juice of one medium lime

Directions:

1. In your big container, toss broccoli slaw mix, cashews, dried cranberries, green onions, and chopped cilantro.
2. In your separate small container, whisk soy sauce, rice vinegar, oil, minced ginger, minced garlic, lime zest, and lime juice until well combined.
3. Pour it over broccoli slaw mixture, then toss well. Serve.

Nutritional Values: Calories: 210; Carbs: 22g; Fat: 11g; Protein: 6g; Fiber: 6g; Sodium 150mg

75.   Cucumber Dill Lentil Salad

Preparation time: 15 minutes
Cooking time: 20 minutes
Servings: 4

Ingredients:

- One cup green lentil, washed
- Two cups water
- One big cucumber, chopped into small pieces
- One-fourth cup each of fresh chopped dill & finely diced red onion
- One medium-sized carrot, grated
- Two tbsp apple cider vinegar
- Two tbsp olive oil, extra virgin
- Juice of half a lemon
- ground black pepper, as required

Directions:

1. In your medium saucepan, add lentils plus water. Let it boil on moderate-high temp, then simmer within 20 mins till lentils are tender. Strain any excess water, then cool it down.
2. In your big container, mix cucumber, dill, red onion, grated carrot, plus cooked lentils.
3. In your separate small container, whisk apple cider, olive oil, lemon juice, plus pepper. Drizzle it over salad, then toss gently. Serve.

Nutritional Values: Calories: 256; Carbs: 30g; Fat: 10g; Protein: 12g; Fiber: 14g; Sodium 37mg

76. Orange Celery Salad

Preparation time: 15 minutes
Cooking time: 0 minutes
Servings: 4

Ingredients:

- Four cups chopped celery
- One big navel orange, peeled and sliced into segments
- Half cup sliced red onion
- One-fourth cup fresh parsley, chopped
- One tbsp olive oil
- Two tbsp apple cider vinegar
- ground black pepper, as required

Directions:

1. In your big container, combine chopped celery, orange segments, sliced red onion, and chopped parsley.
2. In your small container, whisk olive oil plus apple cider till combined.
3. Drizzle it over salad, then toss gently. Flavor it with pepper. Serve.

Nutritional Values: Calories: 87; Carbs: 12g; Fat: 4g; Protein: 2g; Fiber: 4g; Sodium 81mg

77.   Edamame and Corn Salad

Preparation time: 15 minutes
Cooking time: 5 minutes
Servings: 4

Ingredients:

- Two cups frozen shelled edamame, thawed
- One cup frozen corn, thawed
- One cup cherry tomato, halved
- Half cup finely chopped red onion
- Half cup fresh chopped cilantro
- One-fourth cup fresh lime juice
- Two tbsp olive oil
- One-fourth tsp black pepper

Directions:

1. Cook the edamame according to package instructions, making sure not to add salt. Drain and set aside to cool.
2. In your big container, mix cooled edamame, corn, tomatoes, plus onion.
3. In your small container, whisk lime juice, olive oil, plus pepper. Pour this dressing over edamame mixture. Add the chopped cilantro, then toss well. Serve.

Nutritional Values: Calories: 282; Carbs: 29g; Fat: 12g; Protein: 14g; Fiber: 7g; Sodium 30mg

78.   Couscous and Tuna Salad

Preparation time: 15 minutes
Cooking time: 10 minutes
Servings: 4

Ingredients:
- One cup whole wheat couscous, uncooked
- One cup low-sodium vegetable broth
- Half cup cherry tomatoes, halved
- One medium cucumber, diced
- Half cup pitted & chopped Kalamata olives
- One-fourth cup finely chopped red onion
- One-fourth cup fresh chopped parsley
- Five (5 oz each) cans low-sodium tuna, strained & flaked
- One-fourth cup olive oil
- Two tbsp lemon juice
- One tbsp Dijon mustard (check the label for sodium content)
- Ground black pepper, as required

Directions:
1. In your medium saucepan, boil low-sodium vegetable broth. Add the couscous, cover, then remove. Let it sit within 5 mins till couscous has absorbed all broth.
2. Fluff couscous, then transfer it to your big container. Cool it down. Mix in cherry tomatoes, cucumber, olives, red onion, parsley, and tuna.
3. In your separate container, whisk oil, lemon juice, Dijon mustard, plus pepper. Drizzle dressing over salad, then mix well. Serve.

Nutritional Values: Calories: 310; Carbs: 26g; Fat: 15g; Protein: 17g; Fiber: 3g; Sodium 240mg

Sauces and Dressings Recipes

79. Maple Dijon Dressing

Preparation time: 5 minutes
Cooking time: 0 minutes
Servings: 8

Ingredients:
- One-fourth cup apple cider vinegar
- One-fourth cup pure maple syrup
- Two tbsp Dijon mustard (low-sodium)
- Half cup olive oil, extra-virgin
- One-fourth tsp ground black pepper

Directions:
1. In your small container, whisk apple cider vinegar, maple syrup, and low-sodium Dijon mustard.
2. Gradually mix in olive oil, flavor it with black pepper, then whisk for another few seconds. Use immediately or store.

Nutritional Values: Calories: 122; Carbs: 5g; Fat: 11g; Protein: 0g; Fiber: 0g; Sodium 26mg

80. Avocado-Cilantro Dressing

Preparation time: 10 minutes
Cooking time: 0 minutes
Servings: 8

Ingredients:
- One ripe avocado, pitted and peeled
- One cup fresh cilantro, loosely packed
- One-fourth cup plain Greek yogurt (low-fat or fat-free)
- Two garlic cloves
- Juice of one lime
- Two tbsp olive oil
- One-fourth cup water (or more depending on desired consistency)
- Ground black pepper, as required

Directions:
1. In your blender, mix avocado, cilantro, Greek yogurt, garlic, plus lime juice. Blend till smooth. While blending, slowly pour olive oil till fully combined.
2. Gradually add water until you reach the desired consistency. Use more water for a thinner dressing and less for a thicker dip.
3. Season with freshly ground black pepper to taste. Use immediately or store.

Nutritional Values: Calories: 80; Carbs: 3g; Fat: 7g; Protein: 2g; Fiber: 1g; Sodium 10mg

81. Garlic & Herb Greek Yogurt Dip

Preparation time: 10 minutes
Cooking time: 0 minutes
Servings: 6

Ingredients:
- Two cups non-fat plain Greek yogurt
- Two minced garlic cloves
- One-fourth cup fresh parsley, finely chopped
- One-fourth cup fresh chives, finely chopped
- One-fourth cup fresh dill, finely chopped
- Two tbsp lemon juice
- One tbsp olive oil
- Black pepper, as required

Directions:
1. In your medium container, combine Greek yogurt, minced garlic, parsley, chives, and dill. Stir until well-mixed and smooth.
2. Mix in lemon juice plus olive oil, then flavor it with pepper. Serve chilled with your favorite vegetables or low-sodium crackers.

Nutritional Values: Calories: 78; Carbs: 3g; Fat: 3g; Protein: 10g; Fiber: 0g; Sodium 40mg

82. Red Pepper and Tomato Sauce

Preparation time: 15 minutes
Cooking time: 30 minutes
Servings: 4

Ingredients:

- Four big red bell peppers, deseeded and chopped
- Eight ripe tomatoes, peeled and chopped
- One big chopped onion
- Two minced garlic cloves
- Two tbsp olive oil
- One tsp dried basil
- One tsp dried oregano

Directions:

1. In your big saucepan, warm up olive oil on moderate temp. Add onions plus garlic, then cook within 5 mins till tender.
2. Mix in bell peppers, plus tomatoes. Add the dried basil, plus dried oregano. Mix again to combine all ingredients.
3. Adjust to low-moderate temp, then simmer within 20-30 mins till vegetables are soft and well-cooked.
4. Once cooked, remove the saucepan from heat. Blend till smooth using your immersion blender. If you prefer a chunkier texture, blend briefly or just simply mash with a potato masher.
5. Taste your sauce and adjust seasoning if needed or add more herbs as desired. To serve, pour over pasta or use as a base in other DASH-friendly recipes.

Nutritional Values: Calories: 165; Carbs: 22g; Fat: 7g; Protein: 4g; Fiber: 7g; Sodium 25mg

83.   Thai Coconut and Peanut Sauce

Preparation time: 10 minutes
Cooking time: 10 minutes
Servings: 4

Ingredients:
- Half cup unsalted creamy peanut butter
- One (13.5 oz) can of light coconut milk
- Three tbsp fresh lime juice
- Two tbsp low-sodium soy sauce
- One tbsp fish sauce (optional, for a vegetarian version, use additional low-sodium soy sauce)
- Two minced garlic cloves
- One-fourth cup fresh cilantro, chopped
- One-fourth tsp red pepper flakes, crushed
- Two tbsp erythritol

Directions:
1. In your medium saucepan, whisk peanut butter plus coconut milk until smooth.
2. Over medium heat, add lime juice, low-sodium soy sauce, fish sauce (if using), and minced garlic. Stir well to combine.
3. Adjust to low temp, then stir within 5 mins till sauce thickens slightly. Add erythritol or sugar substitute and continue stirring until dissolved.
4. Remove, then stir in chopped cilantro plus pepper flakes. Serve warm over your favorite DASH diet-friendly vegetables, whole grains, or lean proteins.

Nutritional Values: Calories: 259; Carbs: 12g; Fat: 21g; Protein: 10g; Fiber: 2g; Sodium 412mg

84. Raspberry-Balsamic Vinaigrette

Preparation time: 10 minutes

Cooking time: 0 minutes

Servings: 8

Ingredients:

- Half cup fresh raspberries
- One-fourth cup balsamic vinegar
- One-fourth cup olive oil
- Two tbsp water
- Two tsp honey or agave nectar
- One tsp Dijon mustard
- One minced garlic clove

Directions:

1. In your blender or food processor, mix raspberries, balsamic vinegar, olive oil, water, honey or agave nectar, Dijon mustard, and minced garlic. Blend until smooth.
2. Taste and adjust sweetness with additional honey or agave nectar if desired. Pour the vinaigrette into your airtight container, then keep in your fridge for up to one week. Shake well before using.

Nutritional Values: Calories: 63; Carbs: 3g; Fat: 5g; Protein: 0g; Fiber: 1g; Sodium 10mg

Snacks Recipes

85.   Roasted Rosemary Chickpeas

Preparation time: 10 minutes
Cooking time: 30 minutes
Servings: 4

Ingredients:
- Two (15.5 oz each) cans low-sodium chickpeas, drained and rinsed
- One tbsp olive oil
- One tbsp fresh rosemary, chopped
- Half tsp garlic powder
- One-fourth tsp smoked paprika
- One-fourth tsp black pepper, ground

Directions:
1. Warm up your oven to 400°F (200°C). Line your big baking sheet using parchment paper.
2. In your big container, combine drained chickpeas, olive oil, chopped rosemary, garlic powder, smoked paprika, and ground black pepper. Toss to evenly coat the chickpeas with the seasoning mixture.
3. Spread the seasoned chickpeas onto your baking sheet.
4. Roast within 30 mins till chickpeas are crispy. Stir chickpeas halfway through. Cool it down. Serve.

Nutritional Values: Calories: 268; Carbs: 36g; Fat: 10g; Protein: 12g; Fiber: 9g; Sodium 72mg

86. Baked Zucchini Fries

Preparation time: 15 minutes
Cooking time: 25 minutes
Servings: 4

Ingredients:

- Two medium zucchinis, sliced into fries
- Half cup whole wheat bread crumbs (low-sodium)
- One cup grated Parmesan cheese
- One-fourth tsp garlic powder
- One-fourth tsp onion powder
- One-fourth tsp paprika
- One-fourth tsp dried basil
- One-fourth tsp black pepper
- One egg, beaten
- Cooking spray

Directions:

1. Warm up your oven to 425°F (220°C). Line your baking sheet using parchment paper.
2. In your shallow container, mix low-sodium bread crumbs, Parmesan, garlic & onion powder, paprika, dried basil, and black pepper.
3. Dip each zucchini fry into the beaten egg, coating all sides evenly. Coat zucchini fries into the breadcrumb mixture. Put coated fries onto your baking sheet.
4. Lightly spray zucchini fries with cooking spray to help them become crispy while baking. Bake within 25 mins till golden, turning them halfway through cooking for even browning.

Nutritional Values: Calories: 120; Carbs: 16g; Fat: 4g; Protein: 7g; Fiber: 2g; Sodium 85mg

87. Mixed Nuts and Dried Fruit Trail Mix

Preparation time: 10 minutes
Cooking time: 0 minutes
Servings: 10

Ingredients:
- One cup unsalted almond
- One cup unsalted walnut
- One cup unsalted cashew
- Half cup unsalted sunflower seeds
- Half cup unsalted pumpkin seeds
- One cup dried unsweetened cherry
- One cup dried unsweetened apricot, chopped
- One cup dried unsweetened cranberry

Directions:
1. In your big container, mix almonds, cashews, walnuts, sunflower seeds, and pumpkin seeds. Add in the dried cherries, chopped apricots, and cranberries.
2. Mix well until everything is evenly distributed. Serve.

Nutritional Values: Calories: 338; Carbs: 32g; Fat: 22g; Protein: 9g; Fiber: 5g; Sodium 10mg

88. Whole Wheat Pita Chips

Preparation time: 10 minutes

Cooking time: 10 minutes

Servings: 6

Ingredients:

- Six whole wheat pita bread rounds
- Two tbsp extra virgin olive oil
- Ground black pepper, as required

Directions:

1. Warm up your oven to 375°F (190°C).
2. Cut each pita bread round into 8 equal triangle-shaped wedges. In your big container, mix pita wedges, olive oil, plus black pepper.
3. Arrange the seasoned pita wedges on your big parchment paper-lined baking sheet. Bake within 10 mins till golden. Cool it down. Serve.

Nutritional Values: Calories: 197; Carbs: 32g; Fat: 6g; Protein: 6g; Fiber: 4g; Sodium 80mg

89.   Baked Apple Chips

Preparation time: 10 minutes
Cooking time: 2 hours
Servings: 4

Ingredients:

- Four medium-sized apples (preferably a mix of sweet and tart varieties), cored & sliced thinly rounds
- One tbsp lemon juice
- One tsp ground cinnamon
- Cooking spray

Directions:

1. Warm up your oven to 225°F (110°C). Line two baking sheets using silicone baking mat.
2. In your big container, toss the apple slices plus lemon juice to prevent browning.
3. Put apple slices on your baking sheets, making sure they do not overlap. Lightly spray the apple slices with cooking spray and sprinkle with cinnamon.
4. Bake within 1 hour, then flip them over, then bake again within 1 hour until they are crispy. Cool it down. Serve.

Nutritional Values: Calories: 95; Carbs: 25g; Fat: 0g; Protein: 0g; Fiber: 4g; Sodium 2mg

90.   Antipasto Skewers

Preparation time: 20 minutes
Cooking time: 0 minutes
Servings: 6

Ingredients:
- Eighteen cherry tomatoes
- Eighteen small fresh basil leaves
- Eighteen small fresh mozzarella balls, unsalted or reduced-sodium
- Six whole wheat breadsticks or grissini, broken in half
- Six slices of low-sodium deli meat (turkey, chicken, or ham), rolled up
- One cucumber, sliced into thin rounds
- One cup balsamic vinegar reduction, low-sodium

Directions:
1. Assemble the skewers by creating a pattern with a cherry tomato, basil leaf, mozzarella ball, half of a breadstick, rolled-up deli meat, and a cucumber round on a wooden skewer or cocktail stick.
2. Repeat this process until you have used up all the ingredients and created enough skewers for your desired serving size.
3. Lightly drizzle each skewer with the low-sodium balsamic vinegar reduction. Arrange the skewers on a serving platter and keep them chilled until ready to serve.

Nutritional Values: Calories: 300; Carbs: 30g; Fat: 12g; Protein: 18g; Fiber: 4g; Sodium 250mg

91. Sweet Potato Crostini

Preparation time: 15 minutes
Cooking time: 30 minutes
Servings: 6

Ingredients:

- Two medium sweet potatoes, peeled and thinly sliced
- Two tbsp olive oil
- One-fourth tsp black pepper
- One-fourth tsp dried rosemary
- Half cup low-fat ricotta cheese
- One-fourth cup walnuts, chopped
- One-fourth cup fresh chopped basil
- Balsamic glaze for drizzling (optional)

Directions:

1. Warm up your oven to 400°F (200°C).
2. In your big container, mix sweet potato, oil, black pepper, plus dried rosemary until evenly coated.
3. Place the sweet potato slices on your parchment paper-lined baking sheet.
4. Bake within 20 mins, then carefully flip, then bake again within 10 mins till edges are golden. Remove, then cool it down.
5. In your small container, mix low-fat ricotta, chopped walnuts, plus chopped basil. Spread ricotta onto each sweet potato slice. If desired, drizzle balsamic glaze over the crostini before serving.

Nutritional Values: Calories: 190; Carbs: 20g; Fat: 10g; Protein: 6g; Fiber: 3g; Sodium 70mg

92.   Stuffed Celery Sticks

Preparation time: 15 minutes
Cooking time: 0 minutes
Servings: 4

Ingredients:
- Eight celery stalks, washed & cut into three" pieces
- One cup low-fat cream cheese, softened
- One-fourth cup unsweetened Greek yogurt
- Two tbsp fresh chopped dill
- One-fourth cup chopped green onions
- One-fourth cup diced red bell pepper
- Ground black pepper, as required

Directions:
1. In your medium container, mix softened low-fat cream cheese and Greek yogurt. Mix well until smooth and creamy.
2. Mix in chopped dill, green onions, and red bell pepper. Flavor the mixture using black pepper. Mix again.
3. Stuff each celery stick with an even amount of the cream cheese mixture, using a small spoon or piping bag for easier filling.
4. Arrange the stuffed celery sticks on a platter and serve immediately.

Nutritional Values: Calories: 110; Carbs: 6g; Fat: 6g; Protein: 5g; Fiber: 2g; Sodium 190mg

Desserts Recipes

93.   Strawberry Bruschetta

Preparation time: 15 minutes
Cooking time: 5 minutes
Servings: 6

Ingredients:

- Twelve whole-grain baguette slices, toasted
- Two cups fresh strawberries, diced
- One-fourth cup fresh basil, chopped
- One tbsp balsamic glaze
- Four ounces goat cheese, crumbled
- Ground black pepper, as required

Directions:
In your medium container, mix diced strawberries and chopped basil.
1. Warm up your oven to 350°F (175°C).
2. Lay baguette slices on your baking sheet and evenly distribute the crumbled goat cheese onto each slice. Bake within 5 mins till goat cheese has slightly melted. Remove, then cool it slightly.
3. Top each baguette slice with a spoonful of the strawberry-basil mixture. Drizzle lightly with balsamic glaze and sprinkle with freshly ground black pepper to taste. Serve.

Nutritional Values: Calories: 180; Carbs: 24g; Fat: 6g; Protein: 8g; Fiber: 4g; Sodium 190mg

94.   Grilled Pineapple Strips

Preparation time: 15 minutes
Cooking time: 6 minutes
Servings: 4

Ingredients:

- One big ripe pineapple, peeled, cored, & cut into long strips
- Two tbsp fresh lime juice
- One tbsp honey
- One-fourth tbsp ground cinnamon

Directions:

1. Preheat your grill to medium heat or get your grill pan ready on the stove-top.
2. In your small container, mix honey, lime juice, plus ground cinnamon.
3. Put pineapple strips onto the grill or grill pan in a single layer, making sure not to crowd them. Brush the pineapple strips with the lime-honey mixture using a pastry brush.
4. Grill the pineapple strips within 3-5 mins on each side till caramelized. Remove the grilled pineapple strips from the heat and let them cool for a minute before serving.

Nutritional Values: Calories: 110; Carbs: 29g; Fat: 0g; Protein: 1g; Fiber: 3g; Sodium 2mg

95. Lemon Raspberry Yogurt Popsicles

Preparation time: 10 minutes + freezing time
Cooking time: 0 minutes
Servings: 8 popsicles

Ingredients:

- One cup raspberry, fresh or frozen
- Two cups low-fat Greek yogurt, unsweetened
- Three tbsp honey
- Two tbsp lemon juice
- One tbsp lemon zest
- One-fourth tsp pure vanilla extract

Directions:
In your small container, mildly mash the raspberries using a fork to release their juices.

1. In your separate big container, mix Greek yogurt, honey, lemon juice & zest, plus vanilla.
2. Gently fold in mashed raspberries into yogurt mixture without completely mixing them in to maintain a marbled effect.
3. Evenly distribute the yogurt mixture into popsicle molds, filling each mold almost to the top. Insert popsicle sticks and freeze within 6 hours till completely frozen.
4. To remove the popsicles from the molds, run warm water on the outside of the mold for a few seconds and gently pull the popsicle sticks upward.

Nutritional Values: Calories: 90; Carbs: 11g; Fat: 2g; Protein: 7g; Fiber: 1g; Sodium 30mg

96. Blueberry-Oat Bars

Preparation time: 15 minutes
Cooking time: 25 minutes
Servings: 12 bars

Ingredients:
- Two cups quick oats
- One cup whole wheat flour
- Half cup unsweetened applesauce
- One-fourth cup honey
- One tsp vanilla extract
- One cup fresh blueberry
- Half cup low-sodium or sodium-free fruit preserve (blueberry, raspberry, or any preferred flavor)

Directions:
1. Warm up your oven to 350°F (175°C). Line your 9x9" baking pan using parchment paper, then put aside.
2. In your big container, combine oats and whole wheat flour.
3. In another container, mix unsweetened applesauce, honey, plus vanilla extract. Mix it into dry ingredients and mix until well combined.
4. Press half of the oat mixture into the prepared baking pan, creating an even layer. Carefully spread the low-sodium or sodium-free fruit preserve over the oat layer.
5. Scatter the fresh blueberries evenly over fruit preserve layer. Top using rest of oat mixture, pressing it gently onto the blueberries.
6. Bake within 25 mins till top is golden. Cool it down. Slice, then serve.

Nutritional Values: Calories: 180; Carbs: 35g; Fat: 3g; Protein: 4g; Fiber: 4g; Sodium 5mg

97. Spiced Carrot Cake Muffins

Preparation time: 20 minutes
Cooking time: 25 minutes
Servings: 12 muffins

Ingredients:
- Two cups flour, whole wheat
- One cup grated carrots
- Three-fourth cup unsweetened applesauce
- Half cup plain nonfat yogurt
- One-fourth cup honey
- One-fourth cup raisins
- Two big eggs, beaten
- Two tsp baking powder (low-sodium)
- One tsp cinnamon, ground
- One-fourth tsp nutmeg, ground
- One-fourth tsp ginger, ground

Directions:
1. Warm up your oven to 350°F (175°C). Line your standard muffin tin using paper liners.
2. In your big container, whisk whole wheat flour, cinnamon, baking powder, nutmeg, plus ginger.
3. In your separate container, mix grated carrots, applesauce, yogurt, honey, and beaten eggs. Mix it with dry mixture. Fold in raisins gently until evenly distributed.
4. Spoon it into your muffin tin, filling each cup two-thirds full. Bake within 25 mins till golden. Cool it down. Serve.

Nutritional Values: Calories: 150; Carbs: 31g; Fat: 2g; Protein: 5g; Fiber: 3g; Sodium 45mg

98.   Healthy Mixed-Nut Brittle

Preparation time: 15 minutes
Cooking time: 20 minutes
Servings: 12

Ingredients:

- One-fourth cup unsalted almonds
- One-fourth cup unsalted cashews
- One-fourth cup unsalted walnuts
- One-fourth cup unsalted pistachios
- Two tbsp coconut oil
- Half cup of honey
- One tsp vanilla extract

Directions:

1. Warm up your oven to 325°F (163°C).
2. In your big container, mix almonds, cashews, walnuts, and pistachios.
3. In your small saucepan, warm up coconut oil plus honey on low temp. Remove, then mix in vanilla.
4. Pour the heated liquid mixture over the mixed nuts in the bowl and stir until all nuts are evenly coated.
5. Line your baking sheet using parchment paper, then spread the nut mixture out.
6. Bake within 15 to 20 mins till mixture is lightly golden. Cool completely before breaking into pieces. Serve.

Nutritional Values: Calories: 210; Carbs: 17g; Fat: 14g; Protein: 5g; Fiber: 2g; Sodium 20mg

99. Dark Chocolate Almond Date Balls

Preparation time: 15 minutes + chilling time
Cooking time: 0 minutes
Servings: 12 balls

Ingredients:
- One cup pitted date
- One cup raw almond
- One-fourth cup unsweetened dark chocolate chips
- Two tbsp unsweetened cocoa powder
- One tbsp vanilla extract

Directions:
1. In your food processor, process pitted dates till finely chopped. Add almonds, then pulse till combined with a coarse texture.
2. Add in the dark chocolate chips, cocoa powder, plus vanilla extract. Process until a sticky and evenly mixed dough is formed.
3. Scoop out the dough in tablespoon portions and roll them into balls using your hands.
4. Place balls on your parchment-lined plate, then refrigerate within an hour to firm up. Serve.

Nutritional Values: Calories: 150; Carbs: 20g; Fat: 7g; Protein: 4g; Fiber: 4g; Sodium 20mg

100. Fresh Fruit Salad with Mint

Preparation time: 15 minutes + chilling time
Cooking time: 0 minutes
Servings: 4

Ingredients:

- Two cups fresh strawberries, halved
- One cup fresh blueberry
- One cup fresh pineapple chunk
- One cup seedless halved green grape
- One-fourth cup fresh mint leaves, chopped
- Juice of one lemon

Directions:

1. In your big container, combine strawberries, blueberries, pineapple chunks, plus green grape halves.
2. In your small separate container, mix chopped mint leaves plus lemon juice.
3. Pour the mint-lemon mix over the fruit combination and gently toss to evenly coat all the fruit pieces. Chill in your fridge within 30 mins for flavors to meld. Serve cold.

Nutritional Values: Calories: 120; Carbs: 30g; Fat: 1g; Protein: 2g; Fiber: 4g; Sodium 5mg

30-Day's Meal Plan

Days	Breakfast	Snacks	Lunch	Dessert	Dinner
1	Scrambled Egg on Whole Grain Toast	Roasted Rosemary Chickpeas	Roasted Salmon with Maple Glaze	Strawberry Bruschetta	Vegetarian Lasagna
2	Berry Quinoa Breakfast Bowl	Stuffed Celery Sticks	Light Cauliflower-Mushroom Risotto	Fresh Fruit Salad with Mint	Cauliflower and Sweet Potato Curry
3	Strawberry-Ginger Smoothie	Sweet Potato Crostini	Grilled Veggie Skewers with Pesto	Dark Chocolate Almond Date Balls	Penne Arrabiata with Turkey Meatballs
4	Banana Oatmeal with Flaxseed and Almonds	Antipasto Skewers	Lemon Herb Salmon with Asparagus	Healthy Mixed-Nut Brittle	Sesame Ginger Salmon with Bok Choy
5	Spinach and Feta Cheese Frittata	Baked Apple Chips	Brown Rice Vegetable Stir-Fry Bowl	Spiced Carrot Cake Muffins	White Bean and Kale Stew
6	Artichoke Egg Muffins	Whole Wheat Pita Chips	Turkey Swiss Lettuce Wraps	Blueberry-Oat Bars	Turkey and Vegetable Skillet with Quinoa
7	Whole Wheat Apple Cinnamon Pancakes	Baked Zucchini Fries	Hummus Pita Sandwich	Grilled Pineapple Strips	Shrimp Stir-Fry with Brown Rice
8	Mango, Kale & Greek Yogurt Smoothie Bowl	Mixed Nuts and Dried Fruit Trail Mix	Citrus Quinoa Stuffed Peppers Veggie	Lemon Raspberry Yogurt Popsicles	Baked Salmon with Quinoa and Vegetables

Days	Breakfast	Snacks	Lunch	Dessert	Dinner
9	Greek Yogurt Parfait with Honey and Nuts	Roasted Rosemary Chickpeas	Pasta with Pistachio Mint Pesto	Strawberry Bruschetta	Chili Lime Grilled Tofu with Avocado Salsa
10	Overnight Chia Pudding with Fresh Berries	Stuffed Celery Sticks	Spicy Shrimp and Avocado Salad	Fresh Fruit Salad with Mint	Vegetable Pasta Primavera
11	Scrambled Egg on Whole Grain Toast	Sweet Potato Crostini	Roasted Salmon with Maple Glaze	Dark Chocolate Almond Date Balls	Vegetarian Lasagna
12	Spinach and Feta Cheese Frittata	Antipasto Skewers	Light Cauliflower-Mushroom Risotto	Healthy Mixed-Nut Brittle	Cauliflower and Sweet Potato Curry
13	Artichoke Egg Muffins	Baked Apple Chips	Grilled Veggie Skewers with Pesto	Spiced Carrot Cake Muffins	Penne Arrabiata with Turkey Meatballs
14	Whole Wheat Apple Cinnamon Pancakes	Whole Wheat Pita Chips	Lemon Herb Salmon with Asparagus	Blueberry-Oat Bars	Sesame Ginger Salmon with Bok Choy
15	Mango, Kale & Greek Yogurt Smoothie Bowl	Mixed Nuts and Dried Fruit Trail Mix	Brown Rice Vegetable Stir-Fry Bowl	Lemon Raspberry Yogurt Popsicles	White Bean and Kale Stew
16	Overnight Chia Pudding with Fresh Berries	Baked Zucchini Fries	Pasta with Pistachio Mint Pesto	Grilled Pineapple Strips	Turkey and Vegetable Skillet with Quinoa

Days	Breakfast	Snacks	Lunch	Dessert	Dinner
18	Greek Yogurt Parfait with Honey and Nuts	Roasted Rosemary Chickpeas	Spicy Shrimp and Avocado Salad	Strawberry Bruschetta	Baked Salmon with Quinoa and Vegetables
19	Banana Oatmeal with Flaxseed and Almonds	Stuffed Celery Sticks	Veggie Hummus Pita Sandwich	Fresh Fruit Salad with Mint	Shrimp Stir-Fry with Brown Rice
20	Berry Quinoa Breakfast Bowl	Sweet Potato Crostini	Turkey Swiss Lettuce Wraps	Dark Chocolate Almond Date Balls	Vegetable Pasta Primavera
21	Strawberry-Ginger Smoothie	Antipasto Skewers	Citrus Quinoa Stuffed Peppers	Healthy Mixed-Nut Brittle	Chili Lime Grilled Tofu with Avocado Salsa
22	Scrambled Egg on Whole Grain Toast	Baked Apple Chips	Roasted Salmon with Maple Glaze	Spiced Carrot Cake Muffins	Vegetarian Lasagna
23	Mango, Kale & Greek Yogurt Smoothie Bowl	Whole Wheat Pita Chips	Light Cauliflower-Mushroom Risotto	Blueberry-Oat Bars	Cauliflower and Sweet Potato Curry
24	Overnight Chia Pudding with Fresh Berries	Mixed Nuts and Dried Fruit Trail Mix	Grilled Veggie Skewers with Pesto	Lemon Raspberry Yogurt Popsicles	Penne Arrabiata with Turkey Meatballs
25	Greek Yogurt Parfait with Honey and Nuts	Baked Zucchini Fries	Lemon Herb Salmon with Asparagus	Grilled Pineapple Strips	Sesame Ginger Salmon with Bok Choy

Days	Breakfast	Snacks	Lunch	Dessert	Dinner
26	Whole Wheat Apple Cinnamon Pancakes	Roasted Rosemary Chickpeas	Pasta with Pistachio Mint Pesto	Strawberry Bruschetta	Baked Salmon with Quinoa and Vegetables
27	Strawberry-Ginger Smoothie	Sweet Potato Crostini	Brown Rice Vegetable Stir-Fry Bowl	Fresh Fruit Salad with Mint	White Bean and Kale Stew
28	Banana Oatmeal with Flaxseed and Almonds	Antipasto Skewers	Veggie Hummus Pita Sandwich	Dark Chocolate Almond Date Balls	Turkey and Vegetable Skillet with Quinoa
29	Spinach and Feta Cheese Frittata	Baked Apple Chips	Citrus Quinoa Stuffed Peppers	Healthy Mixed-Nut Brittle	Shrimp Stir-Fry with Brown Rice
30	Artichoke Egg Muffins	Whole Wheat Pita Chips	Turkey Swiss Lettuce Wraps	Spiced Carrot Cake Muffins	Vegetable Pasta Primavera

Conclusion

One of the most common ways to lower blood pressure and sugar levels is the Dash diet. The diet is simple to follow and prepare, and it makes use of common grocery store ingredients. However, many people have given up on the Dash diet due to a lack of dish options. Because of this, most people will give up on Dash diet and fall behind until they read this book.

The dash diet should help you feel great, lose weight and have more energy. It's wonderful for ketosis (the process of burning fat for energy) and blood sugar control, and it can keep you regular too! The dash diet is simple and inexpensive. The foods you can eat are delicious, and you don't have to cut out the foods you love. Given the dash diet a try and learn how easy healthy eating can be!

Heart attacks, strokes, heart failure, and some types of cancer can all be reduced with the DASH diet, which has been scientifically demonstrated to be effective. Diabetic complications and kidney stones are both reduced by following the DASH diet plan. The DASH diet emphasises the need of eating a variety of foods while also ensuring that the key nutrients are being consumed in the correct amounts.

Discovering your love for the Dash diet will be easier by following the process given in this one-of-a-kind cookbook. The recipes are suitable for all levels of cooks, from newbies to experts. All you have to do now is follow the recipes offered in the most easy and self-explanatory manner possible, with the most difficult aspects already taken care of.

The recipes and 30-day meal plans in this book cover a wide range of caloric needs for breakfast, lunch, and dinner. The idea is to help you organise your entire month in advance by recognising and appreciating how hectic our lives have become today.

The meals are created to help you stay on track with your Dash diet while also providing your body with the nutrients it requires on a daily basis. In addition to helping, you limit your calorie intake, the meals recommended in the book will also be delicious.

If you stick to the diet's basic principles, you'll rapidly see results. Dash diet recipes can be as simple or as complex as you choose; all you need is a cookbook like this one to get started. You'll become an expert in Dash diet cuisine in no time with these recipes! Nutritious food doesn't have to be tasteless or boring to be healthy. This cookbook teaches you how to prepare delicious meals that are also good for you. If you're looking for a wide variety of recipes that you're sure to enjoy, this book is the one for you.

I'd like to thank you and congratulate you for making it all the way through my lines. Thank you for taking the time to read and consider what I have to say. After reading this book, you should have a clearer picture of the DASH diet. After that, you'll need to gather the appropriate ingredients and test out the recipes in this book. To get the most out of the diet, combine it with regular exercise and a healthy lifestyle. I wish you the best of luck in your endeavours!

Author's Note

Thank you for having read this book, I hope you found it useful.

If you enjoyed the book and have thirty seconds to spare, I would really appreciate a short review on Amazon. Your help in spreading the word is greatly appreciated. Reviews from readers like you make a huge difference in helping new readers find useful information for their needs.

You can use the QR Code or the link below to be redirected to the review page:

Click here to leave a review

Thank you!

Measurement Conversion Chart

Dry measurement (Volume equivalent):

US STANDARD	METRIC (APPROXIMATE)`
⅛ tablespoon	0.5 mL
¼ tablespoon	1 mL
½ tablespoon	2 mL
¾ tablespoon	4 mL
1 tablespoon	5 mL
1 tablespoon	15 mL
¼ cup	59 mL
⅓ cup	79 mL
½ cup	118 mL
⅔ cup	156 mL
¾ cup	177 mL
1 cup	235 mL
2 cups or 1 pint	475 mL
3 cups	700 mL
4 cups or 1 quart	1 L

Liquid measurement (Volume equivalent):

US STANDARD	US STANDARD (OZ)	METRIC (APPROXIMATE)
2 tablespoon	1 fl. oz	30 mL
¼ cup	2 fl. oz	60 mL
⅓ cup	4 fl. oz	120 mL
1 cup	8 fl. oz	240 mL
1½ cups	12 fl. oz	355 mL
2 cups or 1 pint	16 fl. oz	475 mL
4 cups or 1 quart	32 fl. oz	1 L
1 gallon	128 fl. oz	4 L

Weight Equivalents:

US STANDARD	METRIC (APPROXIMATE)`
½ oz	½ oz 15 g
1 oz	1 oz 30 g
2 oz	2 oz 60 g
4 oz	4 oz 115 g
8 oz	8 oz 225 g
12 oz	12 oz 340 g
16 oz or 1 pound	16 oz or 1 pound 455 g

Oven Temperature:

FAHRENHEIT (F)	CELSIUS (C) (APPROXIMATE)
250°	120°
300°	150°
325°	165°
350°	180°
375°	190°
400°	200°
425°	220°
450°	230°

Index

Made in the USA
Monee, IL
06 June 2023